BE SEEN
BE HEARD
BE YOU

THE 10-STEP GUIDE TO PERSONAL BRANDING MASTERY

DHRITIMAN CHAKRABORTY

ISBN
Paperback 979-8-89498-349-3
Hardcase 979-8-89519-867-4

Contents

Strategy 4 - Storytelling: Making Your Personal Brand Relatable 48

Strategy 5 - Networking: Expanding your Personal Brand's Reach 63

Strategy 6 - Online Presence: Digitising Your Personal Brand

x

Preface

My Journey: From a Small Town to Personal Branding Advocate

Life often takes us on unexpected journeys. Mine began in the beautiful town of Tezpur in Assam during the late 70s. Growing up in a small town far from the hustle and bustle of metro cities, I was shielded from the rapid modernisation sweeping across urban India. My family was middle class, and financial constraints meant that the latest technological and cultural advancements were out of our reach. Despite these limitations, my parents instilled in me the values of hard work, education, and integrity, which laid the foundation for my future endeavours.

After completing my management degree, I ventured into the outside world for the first time and visited a metro city. The vibrant city life was overwhelming with its endless opportunities and relentless pace. I felt like a small fish in a vast ocean, struggling to find my place among the sea of corporate professionals. Self-doubt crept in, and I often questioned my abilities and whether I could make a mark in this competitive world.

The Turning Point: A New Direction

My journey continued with numerous challenges and uncertainties until one day, a mentor helped me redefine my life goals. This guidance was the catalyst I needed. I began to view my career from a strategic perspective, and thus, my personal branding journey commenced. It became clear that to grow in my profession and open myself up to new learning opportunities, I needed to make myself visible to the world.

I realised that personal branding wasn't just about promoting myself; it was about understanding and effectively communicating my unique value to others. Over the past two decades, this realisation has been a key focus of my continuous learning. Sharing my insights and experiences has helped me build a personal brand beyond my corporate designation.

Why This Book?

Through this book, I aim to share the strategies I have learned and developed over the past 20-plus years. My goal is to help you build your personal brand and make your mark in the world. Remember, personal branding is not about boasting about your achievements and capabilities. Instead, it's about making yourself visible to those who can benefit from your skills and knowledge. By doing so, you can contribute more to the world and add significant value.

The Importance of Personal Branding

1. **Visibility:** Personal branding ensures that people are aware of your skills and abilities. If no one knows what you are capable

of, you won't be asked to use your talents, no matter how exceptional they may be.

2. **Learning Opportunities:** A strong personal brand opens doors to new opportunities for learning and growth. It allows you to develop your skills and share them with others continuously.

3. **Career Advancement:** Personal branding can accelerate your career growth. It positions you as a leader and an expert, making you more attractive to employers and clients.

4. **Networking:** A strong personal brand attracts like-minded professionals and industry leaders, creating opportunities for meaningful connections and collaborations.

Clarifying the Structure and Intent of This Book

As you embark on this journey through the pages of this book, I want to take a moment to clarify a few key points that will enhance your reading experience and understanding of the strategies presented for building a strong personal brand.

1. **Consistent Chapter Pattern:** You might notice a particular pattern that each chapter follows. This structure is intentional and designed to aid in the better understanding of each strategy. By maintaining a consistent format, the book aims to make complex concepts digestible and relatable on a personal level. This approach ensures that each strategy is not just theoretical but practical and actionable. Additionally, the book provides a few models on some strategies to help you remember a structure while deploying that strategy for your brand-building.

2. **Repetition for Reinforcement:** Throughout the book, you may encounter repetitions of certain points, either within the

same chapter or across different chapters. This repetition is deliberate. The goal is to ensure that key concepts are clearly understood from various perspectives. Repetition helps reinforce the material, aiding in better absorption and retention. When a concept is revisited from different angles, it becomes more ingrained in your understanding, allowing you to apply it more effectively.

3. **Diverse Corporate Examples:** You will find a mix of Indian and global corporate examples used to illustrate the strategies. This diversity is included to provide a broader context and relatability. Whether you are an Indian professional or a global professional, these examples are chosen to ensure there is something relevant for everyone. This mix helps you see how the strategies can be applied universally, regardless of cultural or geographical differences.

4. **Emphasis on Online Tools:** Many strategies in this book are connected to the use of online tools for brand-building. While some readers may prefer not to use these tools due to personal preferences, it is advisable to consider incorporating them into your strategy. The future of personal branding is increasingly digital, and leveraging online tools can help you achieve your goals more efficiently. These tools offer a range of benefits, from expanding your reach to providing valuable insights, and can significantly enhance your brand-building efforts.

5. **Flexibility in Strategy Application:** Although this book presents 10 comprehensive strategies, it is understood that not all may be applicable to every reader. Depending on your area of work and your current position in your brand-building journey, you may choose to focus on only a few of these strategies. The flexibility

to adapt and apply these strategies as per your individual needs is a key aspect of this book. The intention is to provide a toolkit from which you can pick and choose the most relevant tools to help you build and strengthen your personal brand.

My Vision

We are responsible for sharing our knowledge by continuously learning and then disseminating it to others. This not only helps in our personal growth but also contributes to the overall development of society. Personal branding plays a crucial role in this process. It is about making your unique skills and experiences known to the world so that you can make a meaningful impact.

What to Expect from This Book

This book is a comprehensive guide to building and managing your personal brand. It covers everything from the basics of personal branding to advanced strategies for making yourself known in your field. Whether you are just starting your career or looking to take it to the next level, this book will provide you with the tools and knowledge you need to succeed.

A Journey of Continuous Learning

Personal branding is not a one-time effort but an ongoing journey. It requires continuous reflection, adaptation, and growth. The rewards, however, are immense. By investing in your personal brand, you are investing in your future. You are creating opportunities, building a legacy, and making your mark on the world.

I invite you to embark on this journey with me. Let's explore the power of personal branding together and unlock your true potential.

Thank you for joining me on this journey. I hope this book serves as a valuable resource in your quest to build a strong personal brand and achieve your career aspirations.

Introduction

*"Your personal brand is a promise to your clients…
a promise of quality, consistency, competency, and
reliability." – Jason Hartman*

Understanding the Power of a Personal Brand

Opening Anecdote

In 2008, at the peak of the global financial crisis, I found myself at a crossroads in my career. Having spent almost a decade in the corporate world, I was well acquainted with its intricacies, but my professional growth seemed to have plateaued. During this period of uncertainty, I attended a leadership conference in Bangalore. There, a seasoned executive shared his journey of leveraging personal branding to not only survive but thrive amid the economic turmoil. Inspired by his story, I decided to embark on my own journey of personal branding. Over the next few years, I meticulously crafted my personal brand, focusing on my unique strengths and experiences. This transformation revitalised my career and opened doors to opportunities I had never imagined. This book is a culmination of that journey and the lessons learned.

What Has Happened to Personal Branding Over Time

A concept that has become knitted into the very fabric of career advancement is the idea of personal branding, which is a component of professional development. There was a time when a straightforward résumé was sufficient to secure a dream job or climb the corporate ladder. Those days are long gone. As a result of the fact that your online footprint precedes you in this digital era, personal branding has become an essential component of professional success.

Thought leaders such as Tom Peters began to emphasise the significance of personal branding in the early 2000s, which is when the concept of personal branding was first introduced. On the other hand, personal branding did not completely come into its own until the proliferation of social media sites such as LinkedIn, Twitter, and Instagram. Through the use of these platforms, the capacity to construct and exhibit a personal brand has been made more accessible to professionals of all levels, enabling them to promote themselves to an audience on a worldwide scale.

Personal Brand vs. Corporate Brand: Understanding the Distinction

Think of a company's brand as a huge, majestic ocean liner that can be seen from miles away and is driven by everyone's work. On the other hand, a personal brand is like a fast, manoeuvrable ship that moves through the water with its own style and personality. Personal branding is the art of putting together and showing off your own unique mix of skills, experiences, and personal beliefs. Corporate branding is based on the values of a company. It's about making sure that your sailboat is not only safe to sail but also stands out in the water.

Corporate branding is about how a company is known, what it stands for, and what it wants to do. It's about making a consistent picture that customers and other important people can relate to. On the other hand, personal branding is very unique and personal. It's about showing off the skills, experiences, and traits that make you different from other people. When you tell your story, you should make it personal for the people who hear it.

The Indian Corporate Context

India's business world is very active, and personal branding is crucial in this environment. With so many people applying for jobs and the competition being so high, standing out is not only a plus but also a necessity. The Indian way of life, which is full of tradition and variety, adds depth to personal branding, where stories and journeys have a significant impact on how others perceive you and also have lasting effects.

People in India's business world have a unique mix of traditional beliefs and modern goals. This duality makes personal branding both challenging and beneficial. On one hand, there is a lot of respect for established rules and hierarchies. On the other hand, people are becoming more appreciative of new ideas, creativity, and individuality. To navigate this area, you need to find a balance between following cultural norms and staying true to who you are.

The Rise of Digital Platforms and Its Impact

Digital platforms have become the new-age town squares and coffee shops where professional reputations are built and nurtured. A well-crafted LinkedIn profile or a thoughtfully curated Twitter feed can open doors to opportunities that were previously unimaginable. These platforms are not just about visibility; they are about making meaningful connections that transcend geographical boundaries.

LinkedIn, for example, has become the go-to platform for professional networking. It's a place where you can showcase your expertise, connect with industry leaders, and stay updated on the latest trends. Twitter, on the other hand, allows you to share your thoughts, engage in industry conversations, and build a following based on your interests and expertise. Instagram, though often associated with personal and lifestyle content, can also be a powerful tool for showcasing your personal brand, especially if you're in a creative field.

The Components of a Strong Personal Brand

A strong personal brand is built on the pillars of authenticity, visibility, consistency, and differentiation. Like a master chef who knows the perfect blend of spices, a professional must mix these elements in the right measure to create a brand that is both appealing and enduring.

- **Authenticity:** Authenticity is the cornerstone of personal branding. It's about being true to yourself and presenting your genuine self to the world. Authenticity builds trust and credibility, which are essential for any strong personal brand.

- **Visibility:** Visibility is about making sure your brand is seen by the right people. This means being active on relevant platforms, participating in industry events, and continuously engaging with your audience.

- **Consistency:** Consistency reinforces trust. It means that your message, values, and professional demeanour are consistent across all platforms and interactions. Consistency ensures that your audience knows what to expect from you.

- **Differentiation:** Differentiation is about highlighting what makes you unique. It's about identifying your unique selling propositions (USPs) and ensuring they are front and centre in your personal brand.

The Purpose-Driven Brand

At the heart of a compelling personal brand is a clear purpose. When your brand reflects your true motivations and values, it resonates more deeply with your audience, creating connections beyond mere transactions. It's about weaving your personal mission into your professional narrative, making your brand not just seen but felt.

A purpose-driven brand is not just about what you do but why you do it. It's about aligning your personal values with your professional goals. This alignment creates a sense of authenticity and passion that is contagious. It makes your brand more relatable and memorable.

The Benefits of a Personal Brand

A robust personal brand opens a treasure trove of opportunities. It positions you as a thought leader in your field, magnetises professional opportunities, and builds a legacy that outlives conventional career achievements. It's about creating a personal legend that others aspire to.

Some of the key benefits of a strong personal brand include

- **Increased Visibility**: A strong personal brand makes you more visible to potential employers, clients, and collaborators. It ensures that when opportunities arise, you are top of mind.

- **Enhanced Credibility**: A well-crafted personal brand builds credibility and trust. It positions you as an expert in your field and a reliable professional.

- **Career Advancement**: Personal branding can accelerate your career growth by opening doors to new opportunities, promotions, and leadership roles.

- **Networking Opportunities**: A strong personal brand attracts like-minded professionals and industry leaders. It creates opportunities for meaningful connections and collaborations.

Building Your Brand: A Preview

As we embark on this journey together, each chapter ahead will arm you with practical, actionable strategies to sculpt your personal brand. From the art of storytelling to the power of networking, we will explore each facet of personal branding, ensuring you have the tools to craft a brand that not only stands out but also stands the test of time.

Each chapter will delve into a specific strategy, offering step-by-step guidance, real-life examples, and practical exercises to help you apply the concepts to your own personal brand. Whether you're just starting out or looking to refine an existing brand, this book will provide the insights and tools you need to succeed.

Conclusion: The Personal Branding Imperative

Personal branding is your queen on the grand chessboard of professional advancement – versatile, powerful, and game-changing. As we wrap up this introductory journey into the world of personal branding, remember that this is just the beginning. The chapters ahead promise a transformation journey, one where you emerge not just as a player but as a maestro of your professional destiny.

Personal branding is not a one-time effort but an ongoing journey. It requires continuous reflection, adaptation, and growth. By embracing the strategies outlined in this book, you will be well equipped to navigate the dynamic landscape of personal branding and achieve your professional goals.

Chapter 1

Strategy 1 - Self-Awareness: Finding Your Authentic Identity

"If your emotional abilities aren't in hand, if you don't have self-awareness, if you are not able to manage your distressing emotions, if you can't have empathy and have effective relationships, then no matter how smart you are, you are not going to get very far." – Daniel Goleman

Opening Story: The Journey to Self-Awareness

In the bustling city of Mumbai, there was a young professional named Raj who worked as a mid-level manager in a large multinational corporation. Despite his achievements, Raj often felt a sense of dissatisfaction and a nagging thought that he wasn't living up to his full potential. One day, he attended a seminar on personal branding, where the speaker emphasised the importance of self-awareness as the foundation of a strong personal brand. Intrigued, Raj decided to embark on a journey of self-discovery. Over the next few months, Raj engaged in deep introspection, sought feedback from peers, and used various self-assessment tools. This journey not only helped Raj understand his strengths and weaknesses but also uncovered his true passions and values. With this newfound self-awareness, Raj redefined his personal brand, which led to a remarkable transformation in his career and personal life.

The Importance of Self-Awareness in Personal Branding

Self-awareness is the cornerstone of personal branding. It is the process of understanding who you are at your core—your values, passions, strengths, and weaknesses. Without self-awareness, building an authentic personal brand is nearly impossible. It's like trying to construct a building without a solid foundation. Just as Raj discovered, understanding yourself deeply is the first step towards creating a genuine and compelling brand.

Self-awareness helps you align your personal brand with your true self, making it easier to present yourself consistently and authentically across all platforms. It ensures that your brand is not just a façade but a true reflection of who you are. This authenticity resonates with others, building trust and credibility.

The Self-Awareness Journey

Embarking on a journey of self-awareness can be both exciting and challenging. It requires introspection, honesty, and a willingness to confront both your strengths and areas for improvement. Here are some steps and tools to guide you through this journey:

1. **Introspection and Reflection**

   - Set aside time for regular reflection. Think about your career, your successes, and your challenges. What patterns do you notice?

   - Journaling can be a powerful tool for introspection. Write about your experiences, your feelings, and your thoughts.

Over time, you may notice recurring themes that provide insights into your true self.

2. Seeking Feedback

- Ask for feedback from colleagues, mentors, friends, and family. They can provide valuable perspectives that you might not see.

- Use 360-degree feedback tools that allow you to gather anonymous feedback from a variety of sources.

3. Personality Assessments

- Tools like the Myers-Briggs Type Indicator (MBTI), StrengthsFinder, and the Big Five Personality Test can provide insights into your personality traits and strengths.

- Reflect on the results of these assessments and how they align with your own perceptions of yourself.

4. Values and Passions

- Identify your core values and passions. What drives you? What are you passionate about?

- Consider the activities and causes that energise you and bring you joy.

5. SWOT Analysis

- Conduct a personal SWOT analysis (Strengths, Weaknesses, Opportunities, Threats) to gain a comprehensive understanding of where you stand and where you can grow.

Practical Exercises for Self-Awareness

Let's explore some practical exercises that can enhance our self-awareness. These exercises are designed to be engaging and reflective, helping us uncover different facets of our identity.

1. **The Lifeline Exercise**

    - Draw a timeline of your life, marking significant events, achievements, and challenges.

    - Reflect on each event and write down what you learned from it. What strengths did you exhibit? What weaknesses did you uncover?

    - This exercise helps you see the patterns in your life and understand how your past experiences have shaped your present self.

2. **The Five Whys**

    - When reflecting on your goals or challenges, ask "Why?" five times. This technique, known as the Five Whys, helps you dig deeper into your motivations and uncover the root causes of your feelings and actions.

    - For example, if you feel dissatisfied with your job, ask yourself why. Then ask why again to the answer you provide, and so on until you reach a deeper understanding of your underlying motivations.

3. **Mirror, Mirror on the Wall**

    - Stand in front of a mirror and describe yourself out loud. Talk about your strengths, your values, and your passions. Be honest and kind to yourself.

- This exercise helps you articulate your self-perception and can boost your confidence.

4. The Johari Window

- Create a Johari Window, a tool used to improve self-awareness and understanding between individuals. It consists of four quadrants: Open, Hidden, Blind, and Unknown.

- Fill out the Open quadrant with traits you and others are aware of. Fill the Hidden quadrant with traits you are aware of but keep hidden from others. The Blind quadrant is for traits others see in you but you are unaware of, which you can fill after seeking feedback. The Unknown quadrant is for traits that neither you nor others are aware of, which can be discovered through new experiences and self-exploration.

Common Pitfalls in Self-Awareness and How to Avoid Them

While the journey of self-awareness is rewarding, it is not without its challenges. Here are some common pitfalls and how to avoid them:

1. Over-Reliance on External Validation

It's important to seek feedback, but relying too much on others' opinions can skew your self-perception. Balance external feedback with internal reflection.

2. Ignoring Weaknesses

Self-awareness is not just about identifying strengths; it's also about recognising and addressing weaknesses. Be honest with yourself and take proactive steps to improve in areas where you are lacking.

3. Resistance to Change

Self-awareness often leads to the realisation that change is needed. Embrace change as a positive force and be willing to step out of your comfort zone to grow.

4. Superficial Self-Assessment

Avoid the trap of superficial self-assessment. Go beyond the surface and engage in deep, meaningful reflection to truly understand yourself.

The Role of Self-Awareness in Building a Personal Brand

Once you have a clear understanding of your authentic self, you can begin to build a personal brand that truly represents you. Here's how self-awareness plays a pivotal role in this process:

1. Alignment with Values

When your personal brand aligns with your core values, it feels authentic and genuine. This authenticity resonates with others, building trust and credibility.

2. Consistency in Messaging

Self-awareness helps you craft a consistent message across all platforms. Consistency is key to building a recognisable and reliable brand.

3. Clarity in Purpose

Understanding your passions and motivations gives you a clear sense of purpose. This purpose-driven approach makes your brand more compelling and meaningful.

4. Differentiation

Your unique combination of strengths, experiences, and values sets you apart from others. Self-awareness helps you identify and highlight these unique attributes, making your brand stand out.

Real-life Examples of Self Awareness in Personal Branding

- **Virat Kohli**

  1. **Understanding Strengths and Weaknesses:**

     - **Cricketing Skills:** Virat Kohli's journey to becoming one of the best cricketers in the world is a testament to his deep understanding of his strengths and weaknesses. Kohli recognised his natural talent in cricket early on and worked tirelessly to refine his skills. His awareness of his strengths allowed him to focus on becoming an exceptional batsman and leader.

     - **Leadership Qualities:** As the captain of the Indian cricket team, Kohli demonstrated a keen sense of self-awareness. He knew when to assert his authority and when to support his teammates. His leadership style evolved over time, reflecting his understanding of team dynamics and personal growth as a leader.

  2. **Managing Public Image:**

     - **Addressing Controversies:** Kohli's career has not been free from controversies. However, his self-awareness has played a crucial role in managing his public image. He has shown a willingness to acknowledge mistakes and learn from them. This transparency has helped him maintain credibility and trust with his fans.

- **Promoting Fitness and Mental Well-being:** Kohli's emphasis on fitness and mental well-being is another aspect of his self-awareness. Recognising the importance of these elements in his career longevity, he has made them central to his personal brand. His fitness regime and advocacy for mental health resonate with his audience, showcasing a holistic approach to success.

3. **Aligning with Personal Values and Passions:**

- **Consistency:** Kohli's brand is consistent with his values of hard work, dedication, and continuous improvement. He frequently shares his fitness routines and diet plans, emphasising discipline and perseverance. This alignment between his actions and values strengthens his personal brand.

Impact on Personal Brand

- **Global Recognition:** Kohli's self-awareness has helped him become one of the most recognised and respected cricketers globally. His personal brand is synonymous with excellence and leadership in cricket.

- **Business Ventures:** Leveraging his strong personal brand, Kohli has ventured into various business endeavours, including his fitness brand, One8, and collaborations with major brands like Puma. These ventures reflect his commitment to promoting a healthy lifestyle and further enhance his brand's reach.

- **Deepika Padukone**

  1. **Understanding** Personal Struggles:

     - **Mental Health Advocacy:** Deepika Padukone's openness about her struggles with depression and anxiety is a prime example of self-awareness. By acknowledging her mental health challenges, she not only helped herself but also decided to use her platform to advocate for mental health awareness. This decision was rooted in a deep understanding of her personal experiences and the desire to help others facing similar issues.

  2. **Authentic Communication:**

     - **Public Disclosures:** Deepika's candidness about her mental health journey has been a cornerstone of her personal brand. Her public disclosures are genuine and heartfelt, which resonate deeply with her audience. This authenticity has garnered immense respect and admiration, positioning her as a role model.

     - **Consistency:** Her advocacy is consistent across various platforms. Whether in interviews, social media, or public speeches, Deepika's message about the importance of mental health remains constant, reinforcing her commitment to the cause.

  3. **Strategic Use of Platform:**

     - **The Live Love Laugh Foundation:** Deepika founded the Live Love Laugh Foundation to spread awareness about mental health, reduce stigma, and provide support to those affected by mental illness. This initiative showcases her strategic use of her platform to create a significant social impact, aligning her personal brand with a noble cause.

- **Influencing Career Choices:** Her self-awareness and commitment to mental health advocacy have influenced her career choices. Deepika has taken on roles and projects that align with her values, such as the film "Chhapaak," which tells the story of an acid attack survivor. This selective approach to her work further strengthens her personal brand.

4. **Impact on Personal Brand:**

- **Empowerment and Influence:** Deepika's self-awareness has empowered her to use her influence positively. Her advocacy work has not only elevated her brand but also brought about meaningful change in society's perception of mental health.

- **Brand Collaborations:** Her strong personal brand has attracted numerous brand collaborations, where her image of resilience, authenticity, and advocacy for mental health aligns with the values of global brands like L'Oréal Paris and Levi's. These collaborations enhance her visibility and reinforce her brand message.

Conclusion

Both Virat Kohli and Deepika Padukone exemplify how self-awareness can be leveraged to build and sustain powerful personal brands. Their journeys highlight the importance of understanding one's strengths, addressing personal challenges transparently, and aligning actions with personal values. This approach not only elevates their careers but also creates a lasting impact on their audiences and the broader community.

Practical Application: Crafting Your Personal Brand Statement

Now that you have a deeper understanding of self-awareness, it's time to put it into practice by crafting your personal brand statement. This statement is a concise declaration of who you are, what you stand for, and what makes you unique.

Steps to Craft Your Personal Brand Statement

1. **Identify Your Core Values**

   Reflect on your values and what matters most to you. Write down three to five core values that define your character and guide your actions.

2. **Define Your Unique Strengths**

   List your key strengths and skills. What do you excel at? What do others consistently praise you for?

3. **Determine Your Passion and Purpose**

   Think about what drives you. What are you passionate about? What is your purpose in your professional life?

4. **Combine These Elements into a Statement**

   statement that summarises your personal brand. For example, *"I am a passionate leader dedicated to driving innovation and fostering inclusive work environments. My unique strengths in strategic thinking and empathetic communication help me inspire and empower teams to achieve their best."*

5. Refine and Test Your Statement

Share your personal brand statement with trusted colleagues, mentors, and friends. Ask for their feedback and refine it accordingly.

Conclusion: Embracing Self-Awareness as the Foundation of Your Personal Brand

Self-awareness is the bedrock upon which a strong personal brand is built. By understanding your authentic self, you can create a brand that is not only genuine and compelling but also enduring. As you continue your journey of self-discovery, remember that self-awareness is a continuous process. Regular reflection, seeking feedback, and being open to change are essential to maintaining and enhancing your personal brand.

In the next chapter, we will explore the art of differentiation and how you can use it to communicate your personal brand effectively. Through real-life examples and practical tips, you will learn how to craft and share your differentiation story in a way that resonates with your audience and reinforces your brand.

Chapter 2

Strategy 2 - Differentiation: Standing Out from the Crowd

*"In a crowded marketplace, fitting in is a failure.
In a busy marketplace, not standing out is the same as
being invisible." - Seth Godin*

Opening Story: The Differentiation Journey of Deepa

Deepa, a marketing manager in Bangalore, always felt she was just another component in the corporate machine. Despite her hard work and dedication, she often found herself overlooked for promotions and significant projects. One evening, while reading about personal branding, she stumbled upon the concept of differentiation. Intrigued by the idea of standing out, Deepa decided to take a deep dive into what made her unique. Through a combination of self-reflection and feedback from colleagues, she discovered her unique strengths in digital marketing analytics and her passion for sustainable marketing practices. By leveraging these differentiators, she crafted a personal brand highlighting her expertise and resonating deeply with her company's mission. This newfound focus set her apart and led to a series of promotions and speaking engagements at major industry conferences.

Introduction

In today's competitive world, merely being good at your job isn't enough. To truly make a mark, you need to stand out. Differentiation is the key to creating a unique personal brand that sets you apart from others in your field. Unlike storytelling, which focuses on how you convey your journey and experiences, differentiation is about identifying and leveraging what makes you unique. It's about understanding your unique value proposition and making it visible to others.

Why Differentiation Matters

Differentiation is a critical component of personal branding because it allows you to stand out in a crowded marketplace. Here's why it matters:

1. **Visibility in a Crowded Market**

   In today's competitive job market, standing out is essential. Differentiation makes you visible among a sea of professionals with similar qualifications. When employers and clients see what makes you unique, they are more likely to remember and choose you over others.

2. **Highlighting Unique Value**

   By differentiating yourself, you highlight your unique value proposition. This is crucial because it showcases the specific skills, experiences, and perspectives that you bring to the table. This unique value makes you indispensable in your professional field.

3. Creating a Niche

Differentiation helps you carve out a niche for yourself. It allows you to become the go-to person for specific expertise or solutions. This specialisation can lead to higher demand for your skills and services, as people seek out experts who can meet their specific needs.

4. Attracting Opportunities

When you effectively differentiate yourself, you attract more opportunities. This includes job offers, speaking engagements, consulting requests, and collaborations. Opportunities flow towards those who are seen as leaders and innovators in their field.

5. Building a Memorable Brand

A differentiated personal brand is memorable. People are more likely to recall and refer someone who stands out from the crowd. This memorability can lead to word-of-mouth referrals, which are invaluable for career growth and business development.

Here is the edited version of #4:

6. Enhancing Professional Credibility

Differentiation enhances your professional credibility. When you showcase your unique skills and accomplishments, it builds trust and establishes you as an authority in your field. This credibility can lead to greater influence and leadership opportunities.

7. Boosting Confidence and Self-Esteem

Knowing and communicating what makes you unique boosts your confidence and self-esteem. When you are clear about your strengths and value, you can present yourself with conviction and authenticity, which others find compelling and trustworthy.

8. Facilitating Career Advancement

Differentiation facilitates career advancement. Employers and recruiters are always looking for candidates who stand out. By clearly demonstrating how you are different and better, you position yourself for promotions, raises, and career growth.

9. Fostering Innovation and Creativity

Emphasising what makes you different encourages you to continue innovating and being creative. It drives you to constantly improve and adapt, which keeps you ahead in your field and helps you set trends rather than follow them.

10. Encouraging Lifelong Learning

Differentiation often involves continuous learning and personal development. To stay unique, you must keep up with industry trends and acquire new skills. This commitment to lifelong learning not only differentiates you but also ensures your long-term relevance and success.

11. Enabling Better Job Fit

When you clearly define your unique skills and values, you are more likely to find roles and projects that are a good fit for you.

This alignment between your strengths and your work leads to higher job satisfaction and better performance.

12. Increasing Market Value

A well-differentiated personal brand increases your market value. When you offer something that others do not, you can command higher fees, salaries, and better terms in negotiations. Your uniqueness makes you more valuable to employers and clients.

Real-World Examples

Case Study 1: Shantanu Narayen (CEO, Adobe)

Differentiation in Personal Branding

1. Visionary Approach to Digital Transformation:

- **Leadership at Adobe:** Shantanu Narayen's journey at Adobe exemplifies how a clear, visionary approach can set a leader apart. Joining Adobe in 1998, Narayen quickly demonstrated his deep understanding of digital transformation. He played a pivotal role in Adobe's transition from traditional software to a cloud-based subscription model, significantly impacting the company's growth and market position.

- **Foreseeing Market Trends:** Narayen's ability to anticipate and act on market trends differentiated him from other leaders in the tech industry. He recognised the shift towards cloud computing and digital media early on, positioning Adobe to capitalise on these trends. His strategic vision transformed Adobe into a leader in digital media and marketing solutions, driving continuous innovation.

2. Customer-Centric Innovation:

Focus on Customer Needs: Narayen's differentiation strategy involved a strong focus on customer-centric innovation. He led the development of Adobe Creative Cloud, a subscription-based service that provided continuous updates and access to Adobe's suite of creative tools. This customer-focused approach not only enhanced user experience but also ensured a steady revenue stream for Adobe.

- **Fostering Creativity:** Under Narayen's leadership, Adobe fostered a culture of creativity and innovation. He encouraged teams to think outside the box and develop products that not only met current market needs but also anticipated future demands. This culture of innovation set Adobe apart from competitors and established it as a trendsetter in the industry.

3. Continuous Learning and Adaptation:

- **Staying Ahead of Trends:** Narayen's commitment to continuous learning and staying ahead of industry trends played a significant role in his personal branding. He consistently sought new knowledge and insights to drive Adobe's strategic initiatives. His ability to adapt to changing market conditions and lead Adobe through multiple industry shifts reinforced his reputation as a forward-thinking leader.

- **Adaptation to New Technologies:** By embracing new technologies and integrating them into Adobe's offerings, Narayen ensured the company remained relevant and competitive. His proactive approach to technology adoption differentiated him from peers who were slower to adapt.

Impact on Personal Brand

- **Industry Recognition:** Shantanu Narayen's differentiation strategy earned him widespread recognition as a visionary leader in the tech industry. His strategic decisions and innovative approach positioned Adobe as a global leader, enhancing his personal brand.

- **Inspirational Leadership:** Narayen's ability to inspire and lead through change made him a role model for aspiring tech leaders. His journey illustrates the importance of differentiation in building a strong personal brand that is both impactful and enduring.

Case Study 2: Arundhati Bhattacharya (Former Chairperson, State Bank of India)

Differentiation in Personal Branding

1. **Blending Traditional and Modern Practices:**

- **Leadership at SBI:** Arundhati Bhattacharya's tenure as the first woman chairperson of the State Bank of India (SBI) marked a significant shift in the banking sector. Her unique approach to blending traditional banking practices with modern technological advancements set her apart. She focused on modernising SBI's operations while maintaining its legacy of trust and reliability.

- **Digital Transformation:** Bhattacharya spearheaded several digital initiatives, such as the SBI Digital Banking App, which enhanced customer convenience and accessibility. Her ability to integrate digital solutions into traditional banking practices demonstrated her forward-thinking approach and differentiated her from other banking leaders.

2. Customer-Centric Policies:

- **Improving Customer Service:** Bhattacharya's emphasis on customer-centric policies played a crucial role in her differentiation strategy. She introduced measures to improve customer service through technology, such as online banking and mobile banking services. Her focus on enhancing the customer experience set her apart as a leader who prioritised the needs of her clients.

- **Inclusive Banking:** She also promoted financial inclusion by extending banking services to underserved regions. Her initiatives to make banking accessible to all segments of society showcased her commitment to inclusive growth, further differentiating her leadership style.

3. Innovation and Adaptability:

- **Staying Updated with Global Trends:** Bhattacharya's ability to stay updated with global banking trends and incorporate them into SBI's strategy was a key aspect of her personal branding. She actively sought out new technologies and best practices to keep SBI competitive in the global market.

- **Fostering a Culture of Innovation:** Under her leadership, SBI fostered a culture of innovation. Bhattacharya encouraged her teams to develop innovative banking solutions that addressed emerging market needs. This culture of innovation differentiated SBI from its competitors and positioned it as a forward-looking institution.

Impact on Personal Brand

- **Trailblazer in Banking:** Arundhati Bhattacharya's differentiation strategy established her as a trailblazer in the banking industry. Her unique approach to leadership and innovation earned her numerous accolades and reinforced her personal brand as a transformative leader.

- **Role Model for Women Leaders:** As the first woman to lead SBI, Bhattacharya became a role model for aspiring women leaders. Her journey highlighted the importance of differentiation in building a strong personal brand that inspires and empowers others.

Conclusion

Both Shantanu Narayen and Arundhati Bhattacharya exemplify how differentiation can be effectively used to build a strong personal brand. Their unique approaches to leadership, customer-centric innovation, and continuous adaptation set them apart in their respective industries. By leveraging their strengths and staying ahead of trends, they have created impactful personal brands that resonate with a global audience.

Practical Exercises for Differentiation

Let us now delve deeper into actionable practical exercises to achieve an impactful differentiation strategy designed to highlight your unique value and skills:

1. The Strengths Inventory

Self-Assessment:

- **List Your Key Strengths and Skills:** Start by listing all your strengths and skills. Reflect on your career and personal experiences to identify what sets you apart. Think about tasks you excel at, projects where you added significant value, and feedback you've received in the past.

- **Identify Unique Experiences:** Consider experiences that have uniquely shaped your perspective or approach. This could be a particular project, an unusual career path, or a challenging situation you successfully navigated.

- **Feedback:** Seek feedback from colleagues, mentors, and friends. Ask them to identify your strengths and areas where they see you as uniquely valuable. This external perspective can provide insights you might overlook.

Action Steps:

1. Create a detailed list of your strengths, skills, and unique experiences.

2. Ask at least five colleagues or mentors to provide feedback on your strengths and unique attributes.

3. Compare your self-assessment with the feedback to identify common themes and unique strengths.

2. The Unique Value Proposition (UVP) Development

Craft Your UVP:

- **Write a Clear and Concise Statement:** Your UVP should succinctly capture what makes you unique and valuable. It should include your core strengths, the unique experiences that define your expertise, and the value you bring to your audience or clients.

- **Test and Refine:** Share your UVP with trusted colleagues and mentors. Ask for their feedback on clarity, relevance, and impact. Refine your statement based on their input.

Action Steps:

1. Draft a UVP statement that clearly articulates your unique value.

2. Share your UVP with at least three trusted colleagues for feedback.

3. Refine your UVP based on the feedback and ensure it is clear, concise, and impactful.

3. The Market Needs Analysis

Research:

- **Identify Current Trends and Demands:** Conduct thorough research to understand the current trends and demands in your industry. Use industry reports, market analysis, and professional networks to gather information.

- **Look for Gaps:** Identify gaps in the market that align with your strengths and UVP. These gaps represent opportunities where you can apply your unique skills and experiences to add value.

Action Steps:

1. Regularly review industry reports and market analysis to stay updated on trends.

2. Join industry forums, attend conferences, and participate in webinars to gather insights on market needs.

3. Identify at least three market gaps that align with your UVP.

Align Your UVP:

- **Ensure Relevance:** Make sure your UVP aligns with the identified market needs and demands. This alignment ensures that your unique value is relevant and addresses current market challenges.

Action Steps:

1. Adjust your UVP to reflect the needs and demands of the market.

2. Validate your UVP with industry experts or mentors to ensure it is relevant and impactful.

4. The Portfolio Development

Create a Portfolio:

- **Showcase Your Best Work:** Develop a portfolio that highlights your best work and unique skills. Include case studies, project reports, presentations, and other relevant materials that demonstrate your expertise.

Action Steps:

1. Gather your best work samples and organise them into a professional portfolio.

2. Create an online portfolio on your personal website or platforms like Behance or LinkedIn.

Collect Testimonials:

- **Validate Your Achievements:** Gather testimonials from colleagues, clients, and supervisors that validate your achievements and highlight your unique value.

Action Steps:

1. Reach out to previous clients, colleagues, and supervisors for testimonials.

2. Include these testimonials in your portfolio to add credibility and validation.

5. Continuous Learning Plan

Professional Development:

- **Identify Areas for Growth:** Continuously identify areas for growth and seek opportunities for learning and development. This could include formal education, online courses, workshops, or on-the-job training.

Action Steps:

1. Create a professional development plan outlining areas for growth and learning opportunities.

2. Enrol in at least one course or workshop every quarter to enhance your skills.

Adaptability:

- **Be Open to Change:** Stay open to change and be willing to adapt your UVP as needed. The market and industry needs can evolve, and your personal brand should evolve with them.

Action Steps:

1. Regularly review and update your UVP to reflect any new skills or market changes.

2. Stay informed about industry trends and be proactive in adapting your brand strategy.

By following these exercises, you can effectively differentiate yourself and build a strong, memorable personal brand.

Differentiation in the Digital Age

The digital age has amplified the importance of differentiation. With the rise of social media and online platforms, professionals have more opportunities than ever to showcase their unique strengths and build their personal brands.

- **Leveraging Social Media:**
  - Use social media platforms like LinkedIn, Twitter, and Instagram to share your insights, achievements, and experiences. These platforms are powerful tools for building visibility and credibility.
  - Engage with your audience by sharing valuable content, participating in industry discussions, and connecting with other professionals in your field.

- **Building an Online Presence:**
  - It might be a good idea to create a personal website or blog to showcase your expertise and achievements. This platform can serve as a central hub for your personal brand.
  - If interested, you can also use SEO (Search Engine Optimisation) techniques to increase the visibility of your online content. Optimise your website and social media profiles to ensure they appear in relevant search results.

- **Creating Valuable Content:**

  - Share your knowledge and insights through blog posts, articles, videos, and podcasts. Creating valuable content showcases your expertise and builds your authority in your field.

  - At an advanced level, you can use content marketing strategies to reach a wider audience. Promote your content through social media, email newsletters, and collaborations with other professionals and organisations.

The Power of Networking in Differentiation

Networking is a crucial component of differentiation. Building a strong professional network can enhance your visibility, provide valuable opportunities, and reinforce your personal brand.

1. **Strategic Networking:**

   Identify key individuals and organisations in your industry. Build relationships with them by attending industry events, joining professional associations, and participating in online communities.

   Be intentional in your networking efforts. Focus on building genuine relationships rather than simply collecting contacts.

2. **Leveraging Networking Opportunities:**

   Use networking opportunities to showcase your unique strengths and expertise. Share your personal brand story and highlight what sets you apart.

   Offer value to your network by sharing insights, providing support, and collaborating on projects. Building a reputation as a valuable and supportive professional can enhance your personal brand.

3. Maintaining and Growing Your Network:

Stay connected with your network by regularly engaging with your contacts. Share updates, offer support, and show appreciation for their contributions.

Continuously seek opportunities to expand your network. Attend industry events, participate in online discussions, and connect with new professionals in your field.

The Continuous Journey of Differentiation

Differentiation is not a one-time effort but an ongoing journey. As you progress in your career, continuously seek opportunities to learn, grow, and refine your personal brand.

1. Staying Updated with Industry Trends:

- Stay informed about the latest trends and developments in your industry. Continuously update your skills and knowledge to remain relevant and competitive.

- Use industry reports, news articles, and professional development courses to stay ahead of the curve.

2. Adapting to Change:

- Be flexible and adaptable in your approach. The professional landscape is constantly evolving, and your personal brand should evolve with it.

- Embrace change as an opportunity for growth. Be willing to pivot and refine your personal brand as needed to stay aligned with market demands.

3. Seeking Continuous Feedback:

- Regularly seek feedback from colleagues, mentors, and your network. Use this feedback to identify areas for improvement and opportunities for growth.

- Be open to constructive criticism and use it as a tool for continuous development.

4. Celebrating Your Achievements:

- Take time to celebrate your achievements and milestones. Acknowledge your progress and the unique strengths that have contributed to your success.

- Use your achievements to reinforce your personal brand and inspire others in your network.

Conclusion: The Power of Differentiation

Differentiation is the key to standing out in a crowded job market. By identifying and leveraging your unique strengths, you can create a compelling and memorable personal brand. Embrace the journey of differentiation and continuously seek opportunities to grow and refine your personal brand.

In the next chapter, we will explore the concept of building a value proposition and how it can enhance your personal brand. Through practical strategies and real-life examples, you will learn how to create a compelling offer that meets the needs of your target audience and sets you apart in your field.

Chapter 3

Strategy 3 - Building a Value Proposition: Creating a Never-Failing Offer

———— ✸✸ ————

"Your brand is the promise you make; your value proposition is the promise you keep." - John Jantsch

———— ✸✸ ————

Opening Story: The Value Proposition of Anjali

Anjali, a software developer in Hyderabad, was known for her technical skills and dedication. However, she often felt that her team and management did not fully recognise her contributions. During a professional development workshop, Anjali learned about the concept of a value proposition and realised that she needed to articulate the unique value she brought to her projects. She spent time reflecting on her skills and how they addressed the specific needs of her team. Anjali crafted a value proposition highlighting her expertise in optimising software performance, her knack for innovative problem-solving, and her ability to mentor junior developers. By clearly communicating her value proposition, Anjali not only gained greater recognition but also secured a leadership role within her team, significantly advancing her career.

The Importance of a Value Proposition in Personal Branding

A value proposition is the core of your personal brand. It succinctly articulates the unique value you bring to your professional environment and how you meet the needs and solve your audience's problems. Your value proposition is your promise to your potential employers, clients, or collaborators about what they can expect from you.

A strong value proposition in today's competitive job market can set you apart from the crowd. It provides clarity about your unique strengths and the benefits you offer, making it easier for others to see why they should choose you over someone else. A well-defined value proposition helps you communicate your brand consistently across all interactions, from your résumé and LinkedIn profile to interviews and networking events.

Building a compelling value proposition requires a deep understanding of your skills, experiences, and the specific needs of your target audience. It involves more than just listing your qualifications; it's about framing them in a way that highlights their relevance and impact.

Steps to Craft a Powerful Value Proposition

Creating a compelling value proposition involves several steps, each designed to help you identify and communicate the unique value you bring to the table. Here's a detailed guide to building your value proposition:

1. **Identify Your Audience's Needs**

   - Start by understanding the specific needs and challenges of your target audience. This could be your current employer, potential clients, or the broader industry.

   - Conduct research to gain insights into these needs. This can include reading industry reports, attending conferences, and engaging with your professional network.

2. **Highlight Your Unique Strengths**

   - Reflect on your skills, experiences, and accomplishments. What makes you uniquely qualified to meet the needs of your audience?

   - Focus on the strengths that set you apart from others in your field. These could be technical skills, soft skills, or unique experiences that have shaped your professional journey.

3. **Articulate the Benefits You Offer**

   - Clearly define the benefits your strengths provide. How do your skills and experiences translate into value for your audience?

   - Think about the specific outcomes you have achieved in your career. Use quantifiable metrics where possible to demonstrate your impact.

4. **Craft a Clear and Concise Statement**

   - Combine your audience's needs, your unique strengths, and the benefits you offer into a clear and concise value proposition statement.

   - Your statement should be specific, focused, and easy to understand. Avoid jargon and complex language.

5. Test and Refine Your Value Proposition

- Share your value proposition with trusted colleagues, mentors, and friends. Ask for their feedback and use it to refine your statement.

- Continuously review and update your value proposition to ensure it remains relevant and aligned with your evolving career goals.

Real-World Examples of Value Propositions

Case Study 1: A.R. Rahman

1. Blending Indian Classical Music with Contemporary Genres:

A. Musical Innovation: A.R. Rahman's unique value proposition lies in his ability to blend traditional Indian classical music with contemporary genres. This innovative approach has not only revitalised classical music but also made it accessible and appealing to a global audience. His compositions feature a fusion of diverse musical elements, creating a distinctive sound that sets him apart from other composers.

B. Global Recognition: Rahman's work in both Indian cinema and international projects, such as "Slumdog Millionaire," which earned him two Academy Awards, underscores his ability to create music that transcends cultural boundaries. His compositions are characterised by their soulful melodies and innovative arrangements, which have garnered global acclaim and established him as a cultural ambassador for Indian music on the world stage.

2. Championing Social Causes through Music:

A. Promoting Environmental Sustainability: Rahman's compositions often carry messages of unity and compassion. For instance, his work for various environmental causes, including campaigns for water conservation and reforestation, highlights his commitment to sustainability. By integrating social messages into his music, Rahman has expanded his value proposition beyond entertainment, positioning himself as a musician who uses his art to drive positive change.

B. Advocating for Social Harmony: Through his music, Rahman has consistently promoted themes of social harmony and inclusivity. His songs often address issues of peace, tolerance, and mutual respect, resonating deeply with diverse audiences. This holistic approach to music has cemented Rahman's reputation as a composer and visionary whose melodies inspire and unite people across different cultures and backgrounds.

3. Cultural Ambassadorship:

A. Bridging Cultural Divides: Rahman's ability to bridge cultural divides through his music has made him a true cultural ambassador. His collaborations with international artists and participation in global events have further enhanced his personal brand, showcasing the richness of Indian music to the world.

B. Recognition and Awards: His numerous awards and recognitions, including multiple National Film Awards and a Grammy, further solidify his value proposition. These accolades not only celebrate his artistic achievements but also validate his efforts to promote cultural exchange and social harmony through music.

Impact on Personal Brand

Global Acclaim: A.R. Rahman's differentiation strategy has earned him global acclaim and respect. His innovative compositions and commitment to social causes have made him a revered figure in the music industry.

Inspirational Leadership: Rahman's journey serves as an inspiration for musicians and artists worldwide. His ability to create a compelling value proposition through innovation and social advocacy exemplifies how personal branding can extend beyond professional achievements to encompass broader societal contributions.

Case Study 2: Kiran Mazumdar-Shaw

1. Pioneering Biotechnology Innovations:

    A. Entrepreneurial Vision: Kiran Mazumdar-Shaw's value proposition is deeply rooted in her pioneering work in biotechnology. As the founder of Biocon Limited, she has positioned the company as a leading biopharmaceutical enterprise focused on affordable healthcare solutions. Her entrepreneurial journey, from starting Biocon in her garage to transforming it into a global biopharmaceutical giant, highlights her vision and tenacity.

    B. Affordable Healthcare Solutions: Mazumdar-Shaw's commitment to affordable healthcare has set her apart in the biotechnology industry. By focusing on the development of cost-effective drugs and treatments, she has addressed critical healthcare needs in emerging markets, particularly in India. This emphasis on affordability and accessibility has been a cornerstone of her value proposition.

2. Contributions to Scientific Research and Development:

A. Advocacy for R&D: Mazumdar-Shaw has been a vocal advocate for scientific research and development. Under her leadership, Biocon has invested significantly in R&D, leading to breakthroughs in diabetes, oncology, and autoimmune diseases. Her advocacy extends to fostering a culture of innovation within the company and the broader industry, emphasising the importance of research in driving healthcare advancements.

B. Public Policy and Education: Beyond her corporate role, Mazumdar-Shaw has contributed to shaping public policy and promoting science education. She has been involved in various initiatives to enhance the scientific ecosystem in India, including serving on advisory boards and supporting educational institutions. This holistic approach reinforces her value proposition as a leader committed to advancing scientific knowledge and innovation.

3. Empowering Women in Science and Business:

A. Role Model for Women: As one of the few women leaders in the biotechnology industry, Mazumdar-Shaw has become a role model for aspiring women entrepreneurs and scientists. Her success story challenges gender stereotypes and inspires women to pursue careers in science and business.

B. **Mentorship and Support:** She has actively mentored young women and supported initiatives aimed at increasing female representation in STEM fields. Her efforts to empower women align with her broader value proposition of fostering inclusivity and diversity in the workplace.

Impact on Personal Brand

Industry Leadership: Kiran Mazumdar-Shaw's differentiation strategy has established her as a prominent leader in the biotechnology industry. Her innovative approach to affordable healthcare and commitment to scientific research have earned her widespread recognition and respect.

Social Impact: Her contributions to public policy, education, and gender equality have further enhanced her personal brand. Mazumdar-Shaw's ability to leverage her value proposition for broader social impact exemplifies how personal branding can be a powerful tool for driving positive change.

Conclusion

Both A.R. Rahman and Kiran Mazumdar-Shaw exemplify how a well-crafted value proposition can be a cornerstone of a strong personal brand. Their unique approaches to their respective fields, combined with their commitment to social causes, have set them apart as leaders and visionaries. By leveraging their strengths and aligning their value propositions with broader societal goals, they have created impactful personal brands that resonate with diverse audiences globally.

Practical Exercises for Building Your Value Proposition

To help you craft a compelling value proposition, here are some practical exercises:

The Audience Needs Assessment

1. Create a list of the key stakeholders in your professional environment. This could include your current employer, potential clients, or industry peers.

2. For each stakeholder, identify their specific needs and challenges. Consider how your skills and experiences can address these needs.

The Strengths Inventory

1. Reflect on your career and make a list of your key strengths and achievements. Focus on the skills and experiences that have consistently contributed to your success.

2. Seeking feedback is an important aspect of the process. So go ahead and take feedback from colleagues and mentors to identify additional strengths you may have overlooked.

The Benefits Brainstorm

1. For each strength you identified, brainstorm the specific benefits it provides. Think about how your strengths translate into tangible outcomes for your audience.

2. Use quantifiable metrics where possible to demonstrate the impact of your strengths. You may also use any past example from your life for this demonstration.

The Value Proposition Statement

1. Combine your audience's needs, your unique strengths, and the benefits you offer into a clear and concise value proposition statement.

2. Test your statement with trusted colleagues and mentors and refine it based on their feedback.

The Continuous Improvement Plan

1. Create a plan for continuously reviewing and updating your value proposition. Set regular intervals for reflection and feedback to ensure your statement remains relevant and aligned with your career goals.

2. Stay informed about industry trends and evolving needs to keep your value proposition current.

The Role of Collaboration and Networking in Building a Value Proposition

Collaboration is a key element in developing and communicating a strong value proposition. By working closely with others in your field, you can gain new perspectives, gather valuable insights, and refine your unique offerings.

1. Identifying Collaboration Opportunities

1. Look for potential collaborators within your industry, such as colleagues, mentors, and thought leaders. Engaging with diverse professionals can provide fresh ideas and insights to enhance your value proposition.

2. Participate in industry-specific forums, workshops, and conferences where you can meet like-minded professionals who share your interests and goals.

2. Engaging in Meaningful Collaboration

1. Approach collaboration with an open mind and a willingness to learn. Whether you are working on a joint project, conducting research, or sharing knowledge, meaningful collaboration requires mutual respect and a shared vision.

2. Use collaborative projects as a platform to showcase your strengths and expertise. Demonstrating your ability to work effectively with others can significantly boost your personal brand.

3. Showcasing Collaborative Achievements

Highlight successful collaborations in your value proposition. Mention joint projects, co-authored articles, or innovative solutions developed through teamwork. This showcases your ability to collaborate and adds credibility to your personal brand.

Share testimonials and endorsements from collaborators to further reinforce the value you bring to the table. Positive feedback from respected professionals can enhance your reputation and attract new opportunities.

Integrating Feedback into Your Value Proposition

Feedback is an essential component of refining and strengthening your value proposition. By actively seeking and incorporating feedback, you can ensure that your value proposition remains relevant and compelling.

1. **Seeking Constructive Feedback**

   - Proactively ask for feedback from colleagues, mentors, and industry peers. Their insights can help you identify areas for improvement and highlight aspects of your value proposition that are particularly effective.

   - Use structured feedback tools like surveys or one-on-one meetings to gather detailed and actionable feedback.

2. **Incorporating Feedback into Your Value Proposition**

   - Analyse the feedback you receive and look for common themes or suggestions. Use this information to make informed adjustments to your value proposition.

   - Embrace a growth mindset and be open to making changes based on feedback. Continuous improvement is key to maintaining a strong and relevant value proposition.

3. **Communicating Adjustments and Updates**

   - Regularly update your value proposition to reflect any changes or enhancements. Communicate these updates through your online profiles, professional interactions, and marketing materials.

   - Highlight the fact that you actively seek and integrate feedback. This demonstrates your commitment to growth and improvement, further enhancing your personal brand.

Showcasing Your Value Through Content Creation

- Content creation is a powerful way to demonstrate your unique value and expertise in your work area. You can engage your audience and reinforce your value proposition by sharing valuable content.

1. Creating High-Quality Content

- Develop content that showcases your knowledge and expertise. This could include blog posts, articles, videos, podcasts, or presentations. Focus on providing value and addressing the needs and interests of your audience.

- Ensure that your content is well-researched, insightful, and engaging. High-quality content not only attracts attention but also builds credibility.

2. Distributing Your Content Effectively

- Use multiple channels to distribute your content, such as social media, professional networks, and industry publications. The broader your reach, the more people will be exposed to your value proposition.

- Engage with your audience by responding to comments, participating in discussions, and sharing additional insights. Building a relationship with your audience can enhance your personal brand and reinforce your value proposition.

3. Using Content to Highlight Your Unique Value

- Leverage content creation to highlight the unique aspects of your value proposition. Share case studies, success stories, and examples of how you have effectively applied your skills and expertise.

- Use content to demonstrate your thought leadership. Position yourself as an expert in your field by sharing your perspectives on industry trends, challenges, and opportunities.

Leveraging Testimonials and Case Studies

Testimonials and case studies are powerful tools for building credibility and showcasing your value proposition. They provide tangible evidence of your impact and effectiveness.

1. **Gathering Testimonials**

   - Request testimonials from colleagues, clients, and collaborators who can speak to your strengths and the value you provide. Specific and detailed testimonials are particularly impactful.

   - Display these testimonials prominently on your online profiles, personal website, and marketing materials.

2. **Developing Case Studies**

   - Create detailed case studies illustrating how you have successfully addressed challenges and delivered results. Highlight your role, the strategies you employed, and the outcomes achieved.

   - Use case studies to demonstrate your problem-solving abilities, expertise, and the tangible benefits you offer.

3. **Promoting Your Success Stories**

   - Share your testimonials and case studies through various channels, such as presentations, social media, and professional networks. These success stories can reinforce your value proposition and attract new opportunities.

   - Continuously update your testimonials and case studies portfolio to reflect your ongoing achievements and growth.

Focusing on collaboration, feedback integration, content creation, and leveraging testimonials and case studies can help you effectively build and communicate a compelling value proposition. These strategies will enhance your personal brand and position you as a valuable and credible professional in your field.

Conclusion: The Power of a Compelling Value Proposition

A compelling value proposition is the key to standing out in a crowded job market. By clearly articulating the unique value you bring to your professional environment, you can build a personal brand that is both compelling and memorable. Embrace the journey of building your value proposition and continuously seek opportunities to refine and enhance it.

In the next chapter, we will explore the concept of storytelling and how you can use it to communicate your personal brand effectively. Through practical strategies and real-life examples, you will learn how to craft and share your unique story in a way that resonates with your audience and reinforces your brand.

Chapter 4

Strategy 4 - Storytelling: Making Your Personal Brand Relatable

*"Marketing is no longer about the stuff that you make,
but about the stories you tell." - Seth Godin*

Opening Story: The Transformative Power of Storytelling in Raj's Career

Raj, a project manager in Pune, always felt that his professional achievements were overshadowed by his inability to connect with his team and stakeholders on a deeper level. Despite his technical expertise and successful project deliveries, Raj often struggled to inspire and motivate his team. One day, when he attended one of his company events, he observed how his CEO connected with employees by sharing a few personal stories from his professional and personal life. This was the first time that Raj realised the power of storytelling in personal branding. Raj realised that he had been focusing solely on the technical aspects of his job and had neglected the emotional and relational dimensions.

Determined to change this, Raj incorporated storytelling into his professional interactions. He started by sharing personal anecdotes during team meetings, explaining the challenges he had faced and how he had overcome them. He used stories to illustrate his vision for projects and highlight his team members' contributions. Over time, Raj noticed a significant shift in the dynamics of his team. They were more engaged, motivated, and aligned with his vision. By making his personal brand more relatable through storytelling, Raj not only enhanced his leadership effectiveness but also fostered a stronger, more cohesive team culture.

The Importance of Storytelling in Personal Branding

While the concept of Differentiation, described in the previous chapter, helps you to craft a narrative about your differentiating skills and uniqueness, storytelling is a powerful, comprehensive tool that can transform your personal brand from a collection of achievements and skills into a compelling narrative that resonates with your audience.

While the purpose of Differentiation is to highlight the importance of standing out in a crowded market by emphasising unique strengths, skills, and experiences, the purpose of storytelling is to convey how your unique story can be a powerful tool for personal branding by connecting emotionally with the audience.

In the world of personal branding, facts and figures are important, but they are often not enough to create a lasting impact. Stories, on the other hand, have the power to engage, inspire, and connect on a deep emotional level.

A well-crafted story can humanise your brand, making it more relatable and memorable. It can convey your values, vision, and unique strengths in a way that facts and figures alone cannot. Through storytelling, you can share your journey, highlight your achievements, and illustrate how you have overcome challenges.

This not only builds credibility but also fosters trust and connection with your audience.

In today's digital age, where attention spans are short and the competition for attention is fierce, storytelling can set you apart. It can make your personal brand stand out and leave a lasting impression on your audience.

Crafting Your Personal Brand Story

Creating a compelling personal brand story involves several steps. It requires introspection, creativity, and a deep understanding of your audience. Here's a step-by-step guide to crafting your personal brand story:

1. **Identify Key Moments in Your Journey**

   - Reflect on your professional journey and identify key moments that have shaped who you are today. These could include significant achievements, challenges you have overcome, and pivotal learning experiences.

   - Think about the lessons you have learned from these moments and how they have influenced your values, vision, and approach to your work.

2. **Define Your Core Message**

   - Your core message is the central theme of your personal brand story. It should reflect your values, vision, and unique strengths.

   - Consider what you want your audience to remember about you. What key takeaway do you want them to have after hearing your story?

3. Create a Narrative Arc

- A compelling story has a clear beginning, middle, and end. The beginning sets the stage, the middle details the challenges and growth, and the end highlights the outcomes and lessons learned.

- Use vivid descriptions and emotional connections to make your story engaging and relatable.

4. Incorporate Your Unique Selling Proposition (USP)

- Weave your USP into your story. Show how your unique strengths and experiences have shaped your professional journey and contributed to your success.

- Highlight the benefits you offer and how they address the needs of your audience.

5. Make It Authentic and Relatable

- Be genuine and honest in your storytelling. Authenticity builds trust and makes your story more compelling.

- Use relatable examples and anecdotes that your audience can connect with. Share your vulnerabilities and how you have overcome them.

6. Practice and Refine Your Story

- Practice telling your story in different contexts, such as networking events, interviews, and presentations. Refine it based on feedback and observations.

- Continuously review and update your story to ensure it remains relevant and aligned with your evolving career goals.

Real-World Corporate Examples of Storytelling

Case Study 1: Howard Schultz and Starbucks

Storytelling in Personal Branding:

1. **Community and Connection:**

   - **Origin Story:** Howard Schultz, the former CEO of Starbucks, is known for his compelling storytelling that intertwines his personal journey with the Starbucks brand narrative. Schultz often shares his story of growing up in a working-class family in Brooklyn. This narrative not only humanises him but also makes his rise to success relatable and inspirational to many.

   - **Italian Inspiration:** One of Schultz's most influential stories is about his visit to Milan, Italy, where he was inspired by the Italian coffee culture. The experience of seeing how Italians used coffee shops as community hubs profoundly influenced his vision for Starbucks. He envisioned Starbucks as a "third place" between home and work, a welcoming space where people could connect and build community. This story has been instrumental in shaping Starbucks' brand identity and differentiating it from other coffee shops.

2. **Values and Vision:**

   - **Humanising the Brand:** Schultz's storytelling goes beyond just his personal journey. He consistently aligns his stories with the values of community, connection, and resilience. By sharing narratives that reflect his vision and values, Schultz has successfully humanised the Starbucks brand, making it more relatable and trustworthy. For instance, his story about starting the Starbucks College Achievement Plan, which offers full tuition coverage for employees, underscores his commitment to education and employee well-being.

- **Brand Consistency:** The narrative consistency helps in reinforcing the brand's identity. Each story Schultz shares is aligned with Starbucks' mission to inspire and nurture the human spirit. This approach ensures that the brand remains cohesive and its core message is effectively communicated to the audience.

3. Building Resilience:

- **Overcoming Challenges:** Schultz often discusses the challenges he faced in building Starbucks, including his initial struggles to secure funding and the company's early financial difficulties. These stories of overcoming adversity resonate with audiences and build a narrative of resilience and perseverance. This aspect of storytelling not only enhances Schultz's personal brand but also reflects positively on Starbucks, portraying it as a company that has triumphed over obstacles.

- **Cultural Adaptation:** By sharing stories of adapting Starbucks' model to different cultures and markets, Schultz illustrates the company's flexibility and understanding of diverse consumer needs. This adaptability is a key component of Starbucks' global success and a testament to Schultz's visionary leadership.

Impact on Personal Brand

- **Authenticity and Trust:** Schultz's ability to weave his personal experiences with Starbucks' brand story has established him as an authentic and trustworthy leader. His transparency about his journey and the company's evolution fosters a deep connection with consumers and employees alike.

- **Inspiration and Loyalty:**The inspirational nature of Schultz's stories has not only elevated his personal brand but also fostered strong loyalty among Starbucks' customers and employees. By sharing his vision and values through storytelling, Schultz has created a compelling narrative that attracts and retains a dedicated following.

Case Study 2: Richard Branson and Virgin Group

Storytelling in Personal Branding

1. **Adventurous Spirit and Innovation:**

- **Personal Adventures:** Richard Branson, the founder of the Virgin Group, is renowned for his storytelling that blends his personal adventures with the Virgin brand narrative. His daring exploits, such as attempting to circumnavigate the globe in a hot air balloon, are not just tales of personal bravery but also reflect the adventurous and innovative spirit of the Virgin brand. These stories highlight Branson's willingness to take risks and push boundaries, qualities that are central to the Virgin ethos.

- **Breaking Conventions:** Branson's stories often revolve around challenging the status quo and disrupting industries. For example, his narrative about starting Virgin Atlantic to provide a better customer experience in air travel directly confronts the traditional norms of the airline industry. This storytelling approach positions Virgin as a brand that is bold, innovative, and customer-centric.

2. Values and Vision:

- **Empathy and Customer Focus:** Branson's storytelling is not just about his personal adventures but also about his deep commitment to customer satisfaction and employee well-being. His stories about how Virgin companies prioritise customer service and employee happiness reinforce the brand's values of empathy and care. For instance, his narrative about introducing flexible working conditions at Virgin to improve employee work-life balance underscores his forward-thinking leadership and concern for his team's well-being.

- **Inclusivity and Diversity:** By sharing stories that emphasise inclusivity and diversity, Branson has built a brand that stands for equality and social responsibility. His commitment to these values is evident in Virgin's inclusive workplace policies and diverse hiring practices.

3. Relatability and Inspiration:

- **Accessible Success:** Branson's storytelling style is casual, humorous, and highly relatable. He often shares anecdotes about his early business failures and successes in a way that is accessible and engaging. This relatability makes his stories more impactful and inspiring to a broad audience, particularly aspiring entrepreneurs.

- **Visionary Leadership:** Branson's stories consistently highlight his visionary approach to business. By sharing his future-oriented ideas and innovative projects, such as Virgin Galactic's space tourism initiative, Branson positions himself and the Virgin brand at the forefront of innovation and exploration.

Impact on Personal Brand

- **Iconic and Relatable:** Richard Branson's ability to tell engaging and relatable stories has made him an iconic figure in the business world. His personal brand is synonymous with adventure, innovation, and disruption.

- **Engagement and Loyalty:** Branson's storytelling has built a loyal customer base and a dedicated team of employees who resonate with his vision and values. By sharing his experiences and the principles that drive him, Branson has created a strong, cohesive brand narrative that stands out in the crowded marketplace.

Conclusion

Both Howard Schultz and Richard Branson exemplify the power of storytelling in building strong personal brands. Their ability to weave personal experiences with their corporate narratives has not only elevated their brands but also created deep, lasting connections with their audiences. By aligning their stories with their values and vision, they have successfully built personal brands that are authentic, relatable, and inspiring.

Practical Exercises for Developing Your Personal Brand Story

To help you craft a compelling personal brand story, here are some practical exercises:

1. **The Timeline Exercise**

- Create a timeline of your professional journey, marking significant events, achievements, and challenges. Reflect on each event and write down your lessons and how they have shaped your career.

- Use this timeline to identify key moments that can form the foundation of your personal brand story.

2. The Core Message Workshop

- Define the core message of your personal brand story. This should reflect your values, vision, and unique strengths.

- Write a concise statement that captures your core message. Test it with trusted colleagues and mentors and refine it based on their feedback.

3. The Narrative Arc Exercise

- Develop a narrative arc for your story. Start with the beginning (setting the stage), then move to the middle (detailing the challenges and growth), and end with the conclusion (highlighting the outcomes and lessons learned).

- Use vivid descriptions and emotional connections to make your story engaging and relatable.

4. The Authenticity Test

- Share your story with a few trusted colleagues or friends. Ask them for feedback on its authenticity and relatability. Adjust your story based on their feedback to ensure it feels genuine and honest.

- Reflect on your vulnerabilities and how you can incorporate them into your story. Sharing your challenges and how you overcame them can make your story more relatable and impactful.

5. The Practice and Refinement Cycle

- Practice telling your story in different contexts, such as networking events, interviews, and presentations. Pay attention to the reactions and feedback you receive.

- Continuously refine your story based on feedback and observations. Ensure it remains relevant and aligned with your evolving career goals.

Storytelling in the Digital Age

The digital age has transformed the way we tell and share stories. With the rise of social media and online platforms, professionals have more opportunities than ever to share their personal brand stories with a global audience.

1. Leveraging Social Media

- Use platforms like LinkedIn, Twitter, and Instagram to share your personal brand story. Regularly post content that highlights your journey, achievements, and the lessons you have learned.

- Engage with your audience by responding to comments, participating in discussions, and sharing insights related to your field.

2. Creating and Sharing Digital Content

- Share your personal story through blog posts, articles, videos, and podcasts. Focus on creating content that addresses the needs and challenges of your audience.

- Use storytelling techniques to make your content engaging and relatable. Include personal anecdotes, vivid descriptions, and emotional connections.

The Power of Networking in Storytelling

Networking is a crucial component of storytelling. By connecting with others in your field, you can share your story, gain valuable insights, and build relationships that reinforce your personal brand.

1. **Strategic Networking**

   - Identify key individuals and organisations in your industry. Build relationships with them by attending industry events, joining professional associations, and participating in online communities.

   - Be intentional in your networking efforts. Focus on building genuine relationships rather than simply collecting contacts.

2. **Leveraging Networking Opportunities**

   - Use networking opportunities to share your personal brand story. Clearly articulate your journey, achievements, and the lessons you have learned.

   - Offer value to your network by sharing insights, providing support, and collaborating on projects. Building a reputation as a valuable and supportive professional can enhance your personal brand.

3. **Maintaining and Growing Your Network**

   - Stay connected with your network by regularly engaging with your contacts. Share updates, offer support, and show appreciation for their contributions.

   - Continuously seek opportunities to expand your network. Attend industry events, participate in online discussions, and connect with new professionals in your field.

The Continuous Journey of Storytelling

Storytelling is not a one-time effort but an ongoing journey. As you progress in your career, continuously seek opportunities to learn, grow, and refine your personal brand story.

1. **Staying Updated with Industry Trends**

    - Stay informed about the latest trends and developments in your industry. Continuously update your skills and knowledge to remain relevant and competitive.

    - Use industry reports, news articles, and professional development courses to stay ahead of the curve.

2. **Adapting to Change**

    - Be flexible and adaptable in your approach. The professional landscape is constantly evolving, and your personal brand story should evolve with it.

    - Embrace change as an opportunity for growth. Be willing to pivot and refine your story as needed to stay aligned with market demands.

3. **Seeking Continuous Feedback**

    - Regularly seek feedback from colleagues, mentors, and your network. Use this feedback to identify areas for improvement and opportunities for growth.

    - Be open to constructive criticism and use it as a tool for continuous development.

4. Celebrating Your Achievements

- Take time to celebrate your achievements and milestones. Acknowledge your progress and the unique strengths that have contributed to your success.

- Use your achievements to reinforce your personal brand story and inspire others in your network.

Conclusion: The Power of Storytelling

Storytelling is a powerful tool that can transform your personal brand from a collection of achievements and skills into a compelling narrative that resonates with your audience. By sharing your journey, highlighting your achievements, and illustrating how you have overcome challenges, you can build a personal brand that is both relatable and memorable.

In the next chapter, we will explore the concept of networking and how it can enhance your personal brand. Through practical strategies and real-life examples, you will learn how to build and leverage a strong professional network to support your career growth.

By following the strategies outlined in this chapter, you will be well-equipped to craft and share your personal brand story in a way that resonates with your audience and reinforces your brand. Embrace the power of storytelling and let it guide you towards personal and professional success.

In the next chapter, we'll go deeper into the concept of "Networking" and how it can help you build your brand.

Chapter 5

Strategy 5 - Networking: Expanding your Personal Brand's Reach

"Your network is your net worth." - Porter Gale

Opening Story: Rohan's Networking Transformation

Rohan, a mid-level manager in a Mumbai-based logistics company, was a highly skilled professional with a track record of successful projects. Despite his technical prowess and dedication, he felt stuck in his career, unable to break through to higher management levels. He realised that while focusing intensely on honing his skills, he had neglected one critical aspect: networking.

During an industry conference, Rohan attended a session on the power of networking. The speaker emphasised that building relationships could significantly impact one's career trajectory. Inspired, Rohan decided to invest time and effort into expanding his network. He started by contacting colleagues, joining professional associations, and actively participating in industry events. He also leveraged social media platforms like LinkedIn to connect with peers and industry leaders.

Rohan's strategic networking paid off. He began to receive invitations to exclusive industry forums, gained visibility among senior executives, and was eventually offered a leadership role in a prestigious multinational corporation. Through networking, Rohan not only expanded his professional reach but also significantly enhanced his personal brand.

The Importance of Networking in Personal Branding

Networking is a fundamental strategy for expanding your personal brand's reach. It involves building and nurturing relationships that mutually benefit your professional journey. Networking is not just about making connections; it's about creating meaningful relationships that can support your career growth and help you achieve your professional goals.

In today's interconnected world, the power of a strong network cannot be overstated. A robust network can provide access to opportunities, insights, and resources that are not available through formal channels. It can also enhance your visibility and credibility within your industry, making it easier for you to stand out and be recognised for your unique strengths and contributions.

Effective networking requires a strategic approach. It involves identifying the right people to connect with, understanding their needs and interests, and finding ways to add value to the relationship. It also requires ongoing effort to maintain and grow your network over time.

The Networking Process: Steps to Build and Expand Your Network

Building and expanding your network involves several key steps. Here's a detailed guide to help you navigate the networking process effectively:

1. Identify Your Networking Goals

- Start by defining your networking goals. What do you hope to achieve through networking? Are you looking to gain industry insights, find mentors, explore job opportunities, or expand your influence?

- Having clear goals will help you identify the right people to connect with and the best strategies to use.

2. Map Out Your Existing Network

- Create a map of your existing network. Identify your current connections, including colleagues, mentors, industry peers, and social media contacts.

- Analyse your network to identify gaps. Are there key individuals or groups you need to connect with to achieve your goals?

3. Identify Key Individuals and Organisations

- Based on your goals and network analysis, identify key individuals and organisations you want to connect with. These could include industry leaders, potential mentors, influential peers, and professional associations.

- Research these individuals and organisations to understand their interests, needs, and how you can add value to them.

4. Develop Your Networking Strategy

- Create a strategic networking plan. Determine the best ways to connect with your target individuals and organisations. This could include attending industry events, joining professional associations, participating in online communities, and leveraging social media platforms.

- Set specific, achievable goals for each networking activity. For example, aim to meet at least three new people at an industry event or connect with five new professionals on LinkedIn each week.

5. Engage and Build Relationships

- Approach networking with a mindset of *giving rather than taking*. Focus on building genuine relationships by offering value and support to your connections.

- Be proactive in engaging with your network. Attend events, participate in discussions, share insights, and follow up with new connections to nurture the relationship.

6. Leverage Social Media

- Use social media platforms like LinkedIn, Twitter, and industry-specific forums to connect with professionals and engage with your network.

- Share valuable content, participate in discussions, and showcase your expertise through posts, articles, and comments.

7. Maintain and Grow Your Network

- Regularly engage with your network to maintain and strengthen relationships. Share updates, offer support, and show appreciation for your connections' contributions.

- Continuously seek opportunities to expand your network by attending new events, joining additional associations, and connecting with new professionals.

Real-World Corporate Examples of Networking

Case Study 1: Ritesh Agarwal, Founder and CEO of OYO Rooms

Introduction: Ritesh Agarwal's journey with OYO Rooms is a textbook example of leveraging networking to build a global brand. Agarwal, who began his entrepreneurial journey at a young age, recognised the critical role that networking plays in business success. His ability to connect with influential figures in the industry was pivotal in OYO's meteoric rise.

Networking in Action From the outset, Agarwal was proactive in seeking opportunities to expand his network. He participated in numerous startup competitions, which not only honed his business acumen but also put him in touch with key players in the startup ecosystem. One of the most significant milestones in his networking journey was his participation in the Thiel Fellowship, a programme created by PayPal co-founder Peter Thiel.

Thiel Fellowship The Thiel Fellowship provided Agarwal with a platform to connect with a network of entrepreneurs, investors, and mentors. This connection proved invaluable, offering him strategic advice and insights that were instrumental in scaling OYO. The fellowship also opened doors to potential investors who were crucial in securing the funding necessary for OYO's expansion.

Building Strategic Relationships Agarwal's ability to network effectively extended beyond investors. He forged strong relationships with hotel owners, understanding their needs and creating a business model that benefited all stakeholders. These relationships were built on trust and mutual benefit, ensuring long-term collaboration.

Global Expansion Networking played a crucial role in OYO's international expansion. Agarwal's connections helped OYO navigate diverse markets and adapt its business model to local needs. By leveraging his network, he was able to identify and capitalise on opportunities in new markets, making OYO one of the fastest-growing hotel chains globally.

Impact on Personal Branding

Ritesh Agarwal's success story with OYO Rooms underscores the power of networking in building a personal and corporate brand. His strategic connections with investors, industry leaders, and stakeholders were instrumental in transforming OYO from a startup to a global hospitality leader. This case study exemplifies how effective networking can provide the resources, support, and opportunities necessary for business growth and personal brand development.

Case Study 2: Falguni Nayar, Founder of Nykaa

Introduction Falguni Nayar's journey with Nykaa demonstrates how strategic networking can be leveraged to build a successful brand in the competitive beauty and wellness sector. With a background in investment banking, Nayar utilised her extensive network to drive Nykaa's growth and establish herself as a prominent figure in the industry.

Networking Foundations Nayar's career in investment banking provided her with a robust network of industry professionals and investors. When she transitioned to entrepreneurship, she leveraged these connections to gain insights and secure the necessary funding for Nykaa. Her ability to tap into her existing network played a significant role in the initial stages of her business.

Securing Capital One of the critical challenges for any startup is securing capital. Nayar's networking skills were pivotal in attracting investors who believed in her vision. Her connections in the financial industry provided her with access to capital, enabling her to invest in technology, inventory, and marketing, which were crucial for Nykaa's growth.

Industry Connections Nayar's networking extended beyond investors. She actively participated in industry events, conferences, and trade shows, where she built relationships with beauty brands and suppliers globally. These connections allowed Nykaa to offer a diverse range of products, catering to a broad customer base. Her ability to build strong relationships with global beauty brands ensured that Nykaa remained competitive and relevant in the market.

Building Community Networking also played a vital role in building a community around Nykaa. Nayar leveraged social media platforms to connect with customers, influencers, and industry experts. By engaging with her audience and fostering a sense of community, she strengthened Nykaa's brand presence and loyalty.

Impact on Personal Branding

Falguni Nayar's strategic networking was instrumental in Nykaa's success. Her ability to leverage her professional network for funding, industry insights, and partnerships enabled her to build a robust and scalable business model. This case study illustrates the importance of networking in entrepreneurship and personal brand building, highlighting how strategic connections can drive business growth and establish a strong market presence.

Conclusion

Both Ritesh Agarwal and Falguni Nayar exemplify how effective networking can be a powerful tool in building and scaling a business. Their journeys underscore the importance of building strategic relationships, leveraging existing connections, and actively participating in industry networks to drive business success and personal brand development. By strategically utilising their networks, both Agarwal and Nayar were able to secure resources, gain valuable insights, and expand their businesses on a global scale.

Networking in the Digital Age

The digital age has transformed the way professionals network. With the rise of social media and online platforms, connecting with a global audience and building a robust professional network is easier than ever.

1. **Leveraging LinkedIn**

   - LinkedIn is the premier platform for professional networking. Create a compelling LinkedIn profile highlighting your skills, experiences, and achievements.

   - Actively engage with your LinkedIn network by sharing valuable content, participating in discussions, and connecting with new professionals. Join LinkedIn groups related to your industry to expand your reach.

2. Using Twitter for Networking

- Twitter is a powerful tool for networking, especially in real time. Follow industry leaders, participate in Twitter chats, and share insights and updates related to your field.

- Use hashtags to join and follow conversations related to your industry. Engage with others by liking, retweeting, and commenting on their posts.

3. Building an Online Presence

- Create a personal website or blog to serve as a central hub for your professional content. Use this platform to showcase your achievements, share insights, and provide examples of your work.

- You may also optimise your website for search engines (SEO) to increase its visibility and attract relevant visitors.

4. Participating in Online Communities

- Join online communities and forums related to your industry. Participate in discussions, share insights, and connect with other professionals.

- Use platforms like Reddit, Quora, and industry-specific forums to engage with a wider audience and build your network.

The Power of Networking in Building a Personal Brand

Networking is a powerful tool for building and expanding your personal brand. Connecting with others and building meaningful relationships can enhance your visibility, credibility, and influence within your industry.

1. Building Visibility

- Networking can significantly enhance your visibility within your industry. Attending events, participating in discussions, and sharing valuable content can increase your exposure and be recognised as a thought leader.

- You can use social media platforms to amplify your reach and connect with a global audience. Regularly share updates, insights, and achievements to stay top of mind.

2. Enhancing Credibility

- Building relationships with key individuals and organisations can enhance your credibility. When influential figures in your industry endorse or support you, it adds weight to your personal brand.

- Participate in industry events, panels, and discussions to showcase your expertise and build credibility.

3. Expanding Influence

- Networking can expand your influence by providing opportunities to collaborate with others, share your insights, and lead initiatives. By building a strong network, you can become a trusted adviser and leader within your industry.

- Engage with your network regularly to build strong, lasting relationships. Offer support, share insights, and collaborate on projects to expand your influence.

Networking as Part of Your Personal Branding Model

Incorporating networking into your personal branding strategy is essential for expanding your reach and influence. By building and nurturing meaningful relationships, you can enhance your visibility, credibility, and opportunities within your industry.

The Network Influence Model (NIM)

- **NIM**: This model integrates networking as a core component of personal branding. It emphasises the importance of strategic networking, relationship-building, and continuous engagement to expand your personal brand's reach and impact.

Components of the Network Influence Model

1. **Strategic Networking**

   - Identify key individuals and organisations in your industry. Build relationships with them through strategic networking activities, such as attending events, joining professional associations, and participating in online communities.

   - Set specific, achievable goals for your networking activities. Continuously seek opportunities to connect with new professionals and expand your network.

2. **Relationship-Building**

   - Focus on building genuine relationships by offering value and support to your connections. Approach networking with a mindset of giving rather than taking.

   - Be proactive in engaging with your network. Regularly attend events, participate in discussions, share insights, and follow up with new connections to nurture the relationship.

3. Continuous Engagement

- Regularly engage with your network to maintain and strengthen relationships. Share updates, offer support, and show appreciation for your connections' contributions.

- Continuously seek opportunities to expand your network by attending new events, joining additional associations, and connecting with new professionals.

4. Leveraging Social Media

- Use social media platforms like LinkedIn, Twitter, and industry-specific forums to connect with professionals and engage with your network.

- Share valuable content, participate in discussions, and showcase your expertise through posts, articles, and comments.

5. Content Creation and Sharing

- Share your knowledge and expertise through blog posts, articles, videos, and podcasts. Focus on creating content that addresses the needs and challenges of your audience.

- Use content marketing strategies to promote your content and reach a wider audience. Collaborate with other professionals and organisations to expand your reach.

6. Feedback and Improvement

- Regularly seek feedback from your network to identify areas for improvement and opportunities for growth. Use this feedback to refine your networking strategy and personal brand.

- Be open to constructive criticism and use it as a tool for continuous development.

Conclusion: The Power of Networking

Networking is a powerful tool for expanding your personal brand's reach and influence. Building and nurturing meaningful relationships can enhance your visibility, credibility, and opportunities within your industry. Embrace the power of networking and let it guide you towards personal and professional success.

In the next chapter, we will explore the concept of building an online presence and how it can enhance your personal brand. Through practical strategies and real-life examples, you will learn how to optimise your online presence to increase your visibility and impact.

By following the strategies outlined in this chapter, you will be well-equipped to build and expand your network in a way that enhances your personal brand. Embrace the power of networking and let it guide you towards personal and professional success.

Chapter 6

Strategy 6 - Online Presence: Digitising Your Personal Brand

"Personal branding is about making your digital presence reflect your true self, not just your screen time." – Hannah

Opening Story: The Digital Transformation of Meera

Meera, a financial analyst based in Delhi, was well-regarded in her company for her analytical skills and meticulous work. However, she felt that her professional growth was stalling. Despite her expertise, she wasn't receiving the recognition or opportunities she aspired to. A mentor suggested that Meera build her online presence to increase her visibility and showcase her expertise to a broader audience.

Initially hesitant, Meera decided to take the plunge. She started by creating a LinkedIn profile highlighting her achievements and sharing insights on financial analysis trends. She also began writing articles on Medium about industry best practices and participated in relevant online forums. Over time, Meera's online presence grew. She was invited to speak at industry webinars, gained followers who valued her insights and was eventually headhunted for a prestigious role at an international financial firm. By digitising her personal brand, Meera transformed her career trajectory.

The Importance of an Online Presence in Personal Branding

In today's digital era, an online presence is crucial for personal branding. Your online presence is the virtual representation of your professional identity and can significantly impact how you are perceived by colleagues, employers, and industry peers. A strong online presence increases your visibility and enhances your credibility and influence.

Building an online presence involves more than just creating profiles on social media platforms. It requires a strategic approach to showcase your expertise, share valuable content, and engage with your audience. A well-crafted online presence can open doors to new opportunities, from job offers to speaking engagements and collaborations.

A robust online presence allows you to:

- **Increase Visibility**: Reach a broader audience beyond your immediate professional circle.

- **Build Credibility**: Establish yourself as an expert in your field by sharing valuable insights and content.

- **Enhance Engagement**: Connect with industry peers, potential employers, and followers who value your expertise.

- **Leverage Opportunities**: Access new opportunities for career growth, collaborations, and professional development.

The Process of Building an Online Presence

Creating a compelling online presence involves several steps. Here's a detailed guide to help you build and enhance your digital brand:

1. Define Your Online Brand Identity

- Start by defining your online brand identity. Consider how you want to be perceived by your audience and what key messages you want to convey.

- Identify your unique strengths, skills, and experiences that set you apart from others in your field. These will form the foundation of your online brand.

2. Choose the Right Platforms

- Select the social media and online platforms that are most relevant to your industry and target audience. LinkedIn, Twitter, and Medium are popular platforms for professional branding.

- Consider creating a personal website or blog to serve as a central hub for your online presence. This platform can showcase your portfolio, achievements, and thought leadership content.

3. Optimise Your Profiles

- Ensure that your profiles on social media platforms are complete, professional, and consistent. Use a high-quality profile picture and write a compelling bio that highlights your expertise and achievements.

- Use relevant keywords in your profiles to increase visibility in search results. For example, if you are a financial analyst, include terms like "financial analysis," "investment strategy," and "financial modelling."

4. Create and Share Valuable Content

- Share your knowledge and expertise through blog posts, articles, videos, and podcasts. Focus on creating content that addresses the needs and challenges of your audience.

- Use storytelling techniques to make your content engaging and relatable. Include personal anecdotes, case studies, and practical insights.

5. Engage with Your Audience

- Actively engage with your audience by responding to comments, participating in discussions, and sharing insights. Building relationships with your followers can enhance your credibility and influence.

- Join online communities and forums related to your industry. Participate in discussions, ask questions, and share your expertise.

6. Leverage Multimedia Content

- Use multimedia content such as images, infographics, videos, and podcasts to diversify your content and reach a wider audience. Visual and auditory content can be more engaging and shareable.

- Create short videos or podcasts that highlight your insights and expertise. Share these on your social media platforms and website.

7. Monitor and Measure Your Online Presence

- Regularly monitor your online presence to track your progress and measure the impact of your efforts. Use analytics tools to measure website traffic, social media engagement, and content performance.

- Use these insights to refine your strategy and continuously improve your online presence.

Real-World Corporate Examples of Building an Online Presence

Case Study 1: Ravi Venkatesan

Profile Overview:

- Former Chairman of Microsoft India

- Board member of several leading companies

- Active LinkedIn user

Strategy Implementation

1. **Content Sharing:**

   - **Thought Leadership**: Venkatesan regularly shares posts on LinkedIn about leadership, technology, and social impact. His content often includes personal insights, reflections on industry trends, and strategic advice, positioning him as a thought leader.

   - **High-Quality Content**: The posts are well-researched, thought-provoking, and often include data and examples to back his viewpoints. This quality of content attracts a professional audience looking for deep industry insights.

2. **Engagement:**

   - **Consistent Interaction**: Venkatesan engages with his followers by responding to comments, participating in discussions, and sharing relevant industry news. This consistent interaction helps build a loyal following and keeps his audience engaged.

- **Global Reach**: By leveraging LinkedIn's global platform, he connects with a diverse audience, including industry leaders, aspiring professionals, and peers from various sectors.

3. **Visibility and Opportunities:**

- **Speaking Engagements**: His active online presence and thought leadership have led to numerous speaking engagements at conferences, seminars, and webinars. These platforms further enhance his visibility and credibility.

- **Advisory Roles**: His insights and active engagement online have made him a sought-after adviser for various companies. Organisations looking for experienced leaders often reach out to him for his expertise and guidance.

- **Board Positions**: Venkatesan's strong online presence and demonstrated industry knowledge have opened doors to prestigious board positions, as companies seek board members who are well-respected and influential in their fields.

Impact

- **Enhanced Personal Brand**: Through his consistent and strategic online activity, Venkatesan has built a robust personal brand that goes beyond his corporate roles. He is seen as a visionary leader and a trusted voice in the industry.

- **Broader Influence**: His online presence allows him to influence a global audience, share his knowledge, and contribute to discussions on important issues like technology, leadership, and social impact.

Case Study 2: Nisaba Godrej

Profile Overview

- Executive Chairperson of Godrej Consumer Products
- Active on LinkedIn

Strategy Implementation

1. **Content Sharing:**

   - **Business Strategy and Innovation**: Godrej frequently shares her insights on business strategy, innovation, and sustainability. Her posts often include detailed analyses of business trends, strategic initiatives at Godrej, and her vision for the future.

   - **Company Initiatives**: She highlights various initiatives by Godrej Consumer Products, showcasing the company's achievements and her leadership in driving these projects. This helps align her personal brand with the company's brand.

2. **Commitment to Social Causes:**

   - **Sustainability**: Godrej's commitment to sustainability is a recurring theme in her posts. She shares updates on the company's sustainability efforts, innovations in sustainable products, and her personal advocacy for environmental responsibility.

   - **Gender Equality**: She also focuses on gender equality, discussing initiatives aimed at promoting diversity and inclusion within the company and beyond. This reinforces her personal commitment to social causes and aligns with contemporary corporate values.

3. Engagement:

- **Active Participation**: Godrej engages with her audience by responding to comments, participating in industry discussions, and sharing her thoughts on relevant issues. This active participation helps build a strong connection with her followers.

- **Leadership Positioning**: Her posts often reflect her strategic thinking and leadership style, positioning her as a forward-thinking leader in the corporate world.

Impact

- **Enhanced Visibility**: By actively sharing her insights and company initiatives, Godrej has significantly enhanced her visibility in the corporate world. Her online presence ensures that she is recognised as a leader not only within Godrej but also in the broader business community.

- **Strengthened Leadership Position**: Her online activities have reinforced her leadership position, showcasing her as a socially conscious and innovative leader. This not only benefits her personal brand but also enhances the reputation of Godrej Consumer Products.

- **Broader Influence and Opportunities**: Her strong online presence has opened up opportunities for speaking engagements, collaborations, and recognition in various forums. Her influence extends beyond her company, impacting broader discussions on business strategy, sustainability, and gender equality.

Conclusion

Both Ravi Venkatesan and Nisaba Godrej have effectively used their online presence to build and enhance their personal brands. By consistently sharing high-quality content, engaging with their audiences, and aligning their personal brands with their professional goals and values, they have achieved significant visibility and influence in their respective fields. Their strategic use of online platforms demonstrates the power of building an online presence as a key strategy in personal branding.

Leveraging Online Tools and Platforms

Several online tools and platforms can help you build and enhance your online presence. Here are some recommended tools:

1. **LinkedIn**

   - LinkedIn is the premier platform for professional networking and personal branding. Create a complete and compelling LinkedIn profile that highlights your skills, experiences, and achievements.

   - Use LinkedIn to share valuable content, participate in discussions, and connect with industry peers and potential employers.

2. **Twitter**

   - Twitter is a powerful tool for real-time networking and sharing insights. Follow industry leaders, participate in Twitter chats, and share updates related to your field.

- Use hashtags to join and follow conversations related to your industry. Engage with others by liking, retweeting, and commenting on their posts.

3. Medium

- Medium is a popular platform for publishing articles and blog posts. Use Medium to share your insights and expertise with a wider audience.

- Engage with the Medium community by reading, clapping for, and commenting on other writers' articles.

4. YouTube

- YouTube is an excellent platform for sharing video content. Create a YouTube channel to share educational videos, tutorials, and insights related to your field.

- Use storytelling techniques to make your videos engaging and relatable. Promote your videos on your social media platforms and website.

5. WordPress

- WordPress is a versatile platform for creating a personal website or blog. Use WordPress to showcase your portfolio, share your achievements, and provide examples of your work.

- Optimise your website for search engines (SEO) to increase its visibility and attract relevant visitors.

6. Hootsuite

- Hootsuite is a social media management tool that allows you to schedule and manage your social media posts across multiple platforms. Use Hootsuite to streamline your social media efforts and ensure consistent engagement with your audience.

7. **Google Analytics**

- Google Analytics is a powerful tool for tracking and measuring website performance. Use Google Analytics to monitor your website traffic, user behaviour, and content performance.

- Use these insights to refine your strategy and continuously improve your online presence.

The Role of SEO in Building an Online Presence

Search Engine Optimisation (SEO) plays a crucial role in building an online presence. SEO involves optimising your online content to increase its visibility in search engine results. By leveraging SEO, you can attract more visitors to your website and reach a broader audience.

1. **Keyword Research**

- Conduct keyword research to identify the terms and phrases your target audience is searching for. Use tools like Google Keyword Planner, Ahrefs, and SEMrush to find relevant keywords.

- Incorporate these keywords into your website content, blog posts, social media profiles, and other online content to increase visibility in search results.

2. **On-Page SEO**

- Optimise your website's on-page elements, such as title tags, meta descriptions, headers, and image alt text, to include relevant keywords.

- Ensure that your website content is well-structured, easy to read, and provides value to your audience. Use internal links to connect related content and improve navigation.

3. Content SEO

- Create high-quality, valuable content that addresses the needs and challenges of your audience. Use relevant keywords naturally throughout your content.

- Regularly update your content to keep it fresh and relevant. Use a mix of formats, such as blog posts, articles, videos, and infographics, to engage your audience.

4. Technical SEO

- Ensure that your website is technically optimised for search engines. This includes fast loading speed, a mobile-friendly design, and a secure HTTPS connection.

- Use tools like Google Search Console and Bing Webmaster Tools to monitor your website's performance and identify any technical issues.

5. Off-Page SEO

- Build high-quality backlinks to your website from reputable sources. This can include guest posting on other websites, collaborating with industry influencers, and participating in online forums.

- Engage with your audience on social media and online platforms to increase your online presence and drive traffic to your website.

6. Local SEO

- If your personal brand has a local focus, optimise your online presence for local search results. This includes creating a Google My Business profile and using local keywords.

- Encourage satisfied clients or colleagues to leave positive reviews on your Google My Business profile and other review platforms.

Networking and Online Presence: A Synergistic Relationship

Networking and online presence are closely related and can mutually reinforce each other. By combining networking with a strong online presence, you can maximise your personal brand's reach and impact.

1. Leveraging Your Network for Online Presence

- Use your professional network to amplify your online presence. Share your content with your network, ask for feedback, and encourage others to share your content.

- Collaborate with industry peers and influencers to create joint content, such as blog posts, webinars, and podcasts. This can help you reach a wider audience and enhance your credibility.

2. Using Online Presence for Networking

- Use your online presence to facilitate networking opportunities. Engage with your audience on social media, participate in online discussions, and connect with industry peers.

- Share your personal brand story and value proposition online to attract like-minded professionals and potential collaborators.

3. Engaging in Online Communities

- Join online communities and forums related to your industry. Participate in discussions, share insights, and connect with other professionals.

- Use these platforms to build relationships, gain industry insights, and expand your network.

4. Hosting Online Events

- Host online events, such as webinars, live Q&A sessions, and virtual meetups, to engage with your audience and showcase your expertise.

- Promote your events on your social media platforms and website to attract a larger audience.

5. Building a Personal Brand Ecosystem

- Create an ecosystem that integrates your online presence and networking efforts. This includes having a cohesive brand identity across all platforms, consistently sharing valuable content, and actively engaging with your audience.

- Use tools like Hootsuite and Google Analytics to manage and monitor your online presence and networking activities.

Introducing the Digital Presence Influence Model (DPIM)

To provide a structured approach to building an online presence, we introduce the Digital Presence Influence Model (DPIM). This model integrates online presence and networking strategies to enhance your personal brand's reach and impact.

Components of the Digital Presence Influence Model (DPIM)

1. **Define Your Digital Brand Identity**

   - Identify your unique strengths, skills, and experiences that set you apart from others in your field.

   - Define your key messages and how you want to be perceived by your audience.

2. **Choose the Right Platforms**

   - Select the social media and online platforms that are most relevant to your industry and target audience.

   - Create profiles on these platforms and ensure they are complete, professional, and consistent.

3. **Optimise Your Profiles**

   - Use relevant keywords in your profiles to increase visibility in search results.

   - Ensure your profiles highlight your skills, experiences, and achievements.

4. **Create and Share Valuable Content**

   - Share your knowledge and expertise through blog posts, articles, videos, and podcasts.

   - Use storytelling techniques to make your content engaging and relatable.

5. **Engage with Your Audience**

   - Actively engage with your audience by responding to comments, participating in discussions, and building relationships with your followers.

- Join online communities and forums related to your industry.

6. Leverage Multimedia Content

- Use images, infographics, videos, and podcasts to diversify your content and reach a wider audience.

- Create short videos or podcasts that highlight your insights and expertise.

7. Monitor and Measure Your Online Presence

- Regularly monitor your online presence to track your progress and measure the impact of your efforts.

- Use analytics tools to measure metrics such as website traffic, social media engagement, and content performance.

8. Combine Networking and Online Presence

- Leverage your network to amplify your online presence and share your content with your network.

- Use your online presence to facilitate networking opportunities and engage with industry peers.

9. Engage in Online Communities

- Join online communities and forums related to your industry.

- Participate in discussions, share insights, and connect with other professionals.

10. Host Online Events

- Host online events, such as webinars, live Q&A sessions, and virtual meetups.

- Promote your events on your social media platforms and website.

Conclusion: The Power of Online Presence

Building a strong online presence is essential for personal branding in the digital age. By creating and sharing valuable content, engaging with your audience, and leveraging online tools and platforms, you can enhance your visibility, credibility, and opportunities within your industry.

In the next chapter, we will explore the concept of continuous education and how it can enhance your personal brand. You will learn how to stay ahead of industry trends through practical strategies and real-life examples and continuously improve your skills and knowledge.

By following the strategies outlined in this chapter and embracing the Digital Presence Influence Model (DPIM), you will be well-equipped to build and enhance your online presence in a way that supports your personal brand. Embrace the power of an online presence and let it guide you towards personal and professional success.

CONTINUE
EDUCATE EDUCATION

Strategy 7 - Continuous Education: Learning as a Lifelong Endeavour

"Live as if you were to die tomorrow. Learn as if you were to live forever." – Mahatma Gandhi

Opening Story: Ravi's Journey of Lifelong Learning

Ravi, an IT professional based in Bangalore, had always been known for his technical expertise and dedication. However, as the technology landscape evolved rapidly, Ravi began to feel that his skills were becoming outdated. He noticed younger colleagues who were adept at new technologies and methodologies gaining recognition and advancing faster in their careers. Determined to stay relevant, Ravi decided to embrace continuous education.

He started by enrolling in online courses and certifications related to emerging technologies like artificial intelligence, machine learning, and cloud computing. Ravi also attended industry conferences and workshops to learn from experts and network with peers. Over time, his efforts paid off. Ravi not only updated his skillset but also gained a reputation as an innovator and thought leader in his company. He was invited to lead high-profile projects and was eventually promoted to a senior management position.

By committing to lifelong learning, Ravi stayed relevant and significantly advanced his career.

The Importance of Continuous Education in Personal Branding

In today's fast-paced and ever-changing professional landscape, continuous education is crucial for personal branding. Lifelong learning ensures that you remain relevant, competitive, and adaptable in your field. It allows you to stay ahead of industry trends, acquire new skills, and demonstrate a commitment to personal and professional growth.

Continuous education is not just about acquiring new knowledge; it's about cultivating a mindset of curiosity and adaptability. It involves seeking out opportunities for learning and growth, whether through formal education, self-study, or experiential learning. By continuously updating your skills and knowledge, you can enhance your personal brand, increase your value to employers, and open doors to new opportunities.

Benefits of continuous education include:

- **Staying Relevant**: Keeping up with industry trends and advancements to remain competitive.

- **Enhancing Expertise**: Expanding your knowledge and skills to become a subject matter expert.

- **Demonstrating Commitment**: Showing employers and colleagues that you are dedicated to continuous improvement.

- **Increasing Opportunities**: Accessing new career opportunities, promotions, and professional growth.

The Process of Embracing Continuous Education

Embracing continuous education involves several steps. Here's a detailed guide to help you integrate lifelong learning into your personal and professional development:

1. **Identify Your Learning Goals**

   - Start by identifying your learning goals. Consider what skills and knowledge you need to stay relevant and competitive in your field.

   - Reflect on your career aspirations and identify areas for growth or improvement. Set specific, achievable learning objectives that align with your goals.

2. **Research Learning Opportunities**

   - Research various learning opportunities that align with your goals. This can include formal education programmes, online courses, certifications, workshops, conferences, and self-study resources.

   - Look for reputable institutions and platforms that offer high-quality learning experiences. Consider factors such as course content, instructor expertise, and student reviews.

3. **Create a Learning Plan**

   - Develop a learning plan that outlines the steps you will take to achieve your learning goals. Include specific courses, programmes, and activities you will participate in, along with timelines and milestones.

   - Schedule a regular time for learning in your calendar. Treat it as a priority and commit to a consistent, ongoing effort.

4. Engage in Experiential Learning

- Seek out opportunities for experiential learning, such as internships, volunteer work, and on-the-job training. These experiences can provide hands-on learning and practical application of new skills.

- Participate in industry events, conferences, and workshops to learn from experts and network with peers. These experiences can also provide valuable insights and inspiration.

5. Leverage Online Learning Platforms

- Take advantage of online learning platforms that offer a wide range of courses and certifications. Platforms like Coursera, edX, Udemy, and LinkedIn Learning provide access to high-quality content from top institutions and instructors.

- Use these platforms to learn at your own pace and on your own schedule. Many courses offer flexible options that allow you to balance learning with work and other commitments.

6. Seek Mentorship and Coaching

- Find mentors and coaches who can provide guidance, support, and feedback on your learning journey. Mentors can offer valuable insights, share their experiences, and help you navigate challenges.

- Join professional associations and networking groups to connect with potential mentors and peers who share your learning goals.

7. Reflect and Apply Your Learning

- Regularly reflect on your learning experiences and assess your progress. Consider what you have learned, how it applies to your work, and how it aligns with your goals.

- Apply your new knowledge and skills in your professional environment. Look for opportunities to use what you have learned to solve problems, innovate, and contribute to your organisation's success.

Real-World Corporate Examples of Continuous Education

Case Study 1

Harsh Mariwala, Chairman of Marico Limited

Profile Overview

- Chairman of Marico Limited
- Transformed a family trading business into a leading FMCG company

Strategy Implementation

1. **Commitment to Continuous Learning:**

   - **Management Programmes**: Harsh Mariwala has attended several management programmes, including those at prestigious institutions like Harvard Business School. These programmes have provided him with advanced business knowledge and strategic insights that he has applied to Marico's growth.

   - **Industry Trends**: He continuously updates himself on the latest trends in the FMCG sector, from consumer behaviour to technological advancements. This proactive approach ensures that Marico stays competitive in a rapidly evolving market.

2. **Fostering a Learning Culture:**

   - **Employee Development**: Mariwala emphasises the importance of continuous education for his employees. He has implemented programmes that encourage Marico's workforce to pursue further education and professional development. This culture of learning helps the company innovate and adapt to changes more effectively.

   - **Learning Platforms**: Marico provides various platforms and resources for employees to upgrade their skills, such as e-learning modules, workshops, and access to industry seminars.

3. **Adapting Business Strategies:**

   - **Market Adaptation**: Mariwala's commitment to learning has enabled him to adapt Marico's business strategies to meet changing market demands. Whether it's entering new markets or innovating product lines, his ability to leverage new knowledge has been crucial.

   - **Strategic Partnerships**: By staying informed about global best practices, Mariwala has been able to forge strategic partnerships that align with Marico's growth objectives.

Impact

   - **Enhanced Corporate Performance**: Mariwala's continuous learning has directly contributed to Marico's success, driving innovation and market expansion.

   - **Leadership Brand**: His dedication to learning positions him as a forward-thinking leader who values growth and development, enhancing his personal brand and that of Marico.

Case Study 2

Radhakishan Damani, Founder of DMart

Profile Overview

- Founder of DMart

- Known as the "retail king of India" and "Warren Buffet of India"

- Self-made billionaire with humble beginnings

Strategy Implementation

1. Humble Beginnings:

- **Early Career**: Radhakishan Damani started his career with a modest education, dropping out of college after just one year. Initially, he worked as a ball-bearing trader and later entered the stock market, where he made his mark as a successful investor.

2. Continuous Learning on the Job:

- **Stock Market Insights**: Despite limited formal education, Damani leveraged his keen observational skills and willingness to learn from market trends and experienced investors. His practical learning in the stock market provided a strong foundation for his future ventures.

- **Retail Industry Mastery**: Transitioning from stock market investments to retail, Damani applied what he had learned from observing market demands and consumer behaviour. He meticulously studied retail models and strategies, both in India and internationally, which helped him conceptualise DMart.

3. Building a Personal Brand:

- **Simple Lifestyle:** Known for his simplicity and low profile, Damani's personal brand is built on humility and integrity. He maintains a simple lifestyle, often seen in plain white attire, which resonates with his straightforward business ethos.

- **Strategic Vision:** His ability to adapt and continuously learn has been pivotal in DMart's success. By focusing on efficient operations, cost-effective pricing, and understanding customer needs, Damani has built a strong, trustworthy brand in the competitive retail sector.

Impact

- **Corporate Success:** Under Damani's leadership, DMart has grown into one of India's leading retail chains, known for its cost efficiency and customer-centric approach. His strategies have made DMart a highly profitable and respected company in the Indian retail market.

- **Enhanced Personal Brand:** Damani's journey from humble beginnings to becoming a billionaire highlights the power of continuous learning and adaptation. His success story serves as an inspiration for many aspiring entrepreneurs, reinforcing the value of practical knowledge and persistent effort.

Practical Exercises for Embracing Continuous Education

To help you integrate continuous education into your personal and professional development, here are some practical exercises designed to foster lifelong learning:

1. The Learning Goals Worksheet

- **Identify Learning Goals:**
  - Reflect on your career aspirations and areas for growth.
  - Write down specific skills and knowledge you need to stay relevant and competitive in your field.

- **Set Clear Objectives:**
  - Establish short-term and long-term learning objectives that align with your career goals.
  - Ensure these objectives are specific, measurable, achievable, relevant, and time-bound (SMART).

2. The Learning Opportunities Research

- **Research Learning Opportunities:**
  - Identify various learning opportunities that align with your goals.
  - Create a list of formal education programmes, online courses, certifications, workshops, conferences, and self-study resources.

- **Evaluate Quality and Relevance:**
  - Assess the quality and relevance of each learning opportunity.
  - Consider factors such as course content, instructor expertise, and student reviews.

3. The Learning Plan Development

- **Develop a Comprehensive Learning Plan:**
  - Outline the steps you will take to achieve your learning goals.

- Include specific courses, programmes, and activities, along with timelines and milestones.
- **Schedule Regular Learning Time:**
  - Allocate regular time in your calendar for learning.
  - Treat it as a priority and commit to a consistent, ongoing effort.

4. The Experiential Learning Exercise

- **Seek Experiential Learning Opportunities:**
  - Pursue internships, volunteer work, and on-the-job training.
  - Identify experiences that offer hands-on learning and practical application of new skills.
- **Participate in Industry Events:**
  - Attend conferences, workshops, and seminars to learn from experts and network with peers.
  - Document your experiences and reflect on your learnings.

5. The Online Learning Strategy

- **Leverage Online Platforms:**
  - Use platforms like Coursera, edX, Udemy, LinkedIn Learning, Khan Academy, and Google Skillshop.
  - Access high-quality content from top institutions and instructors.
- **Set Specific Course Goals:**
  - Establish goals for each course and track your progress.
  - Balance your studies with work and other commitments using the flexibility of online learning.

6. The Mentorship and Coaching Plan

- **Find Mentors and Coaches:**
  - Seek guidance, support, and feedback from mentors within your professional network.
  - Join professional associations and networking groups to connect with peers who share your learning goals.

- **Participate in Mentorship Programmes:**
  - Engage in formal mentorship programmes offered by organisations and associations.

7. The Reflection and Application Journal

- **Reflect on Learning Experiences:**
  - Regularly assess your progress and document what you have learned.
  - Create a journal to track how new knowledge and skills apply to your work and align with your goals.

- **Identify Application Opportunities:**
  - Look for ways to apply your new knowledge and skills in your professional environment.
  - Use your learnings to solve problems, innovate, and contribute to your organisation's success.

Leveraging Online Learning Platforms

Several online learning platforms offer a wide range of courses and certifications to support continuous education. Here are some recommended platforms:

1. **Coursera**

   - **Courses and Certifications:**
     - Offers courses from top universities and institutions worldwide.
     - Subjects range from business and technology to arts and humanities.
   - **Flexible Learning:**
     - Learn at your own pace and earn recognised credentials.

2. **edX**

   - **Access to Leading Universities:**
     - Provides courses from leading universities and organisations.
     - Subjects include computer science, data science, engineering, and more.
   - **Interactive Content:**
     - Enhance your skills with flexible learning options and interactive content.

3. **Udemy**

   - **Vast Library of Courses:**
     - Offers a wide range of courses on subjects like programming, marketing, personal development, and more.
     - Courses are created by industry experts and practitioners.
   - **Explore New Skills:**
     - Learn new skills, improve existing ones, and explore new areas of interest.

4. LinkedIn Learning

- **Business, Technology, and Creative Skills:**
  - Provides access to courses and tutorials taught by industry professionals.
  - Integrated with LinkedIn profiles to enhance your professional visibility.
- **Stay Updated:**
  - Keep up with industry trends and gain new skills.

5. Khan Academy

- **Free Educational Resources:**
  - Offers courses on subjects like math, science, economics, and more.
  - Suitable for learners of all ages and levels.
- **Build Foundational Knowledge:**
  - Explore new subjects at no cost.

6. Google Skillshop

- **Training on Google Products:**
  - Provides free training and certifications on Google products and tools.
  - Includes Google Ads, Analytics, and Cloud.
- **Gain Expertise:**
  - Develop skills in digital marketing, data analysis, and cloud computing.

The Personal Brand Enhancement Model (PBEM)

The Personal Brand Enhancement Model (PBEM) provides a unique framework for integrating continuous education with personal and professional development. This model emphasises strategic personal brand enhancement through lifelong learning.

Components of the Personal Brand Enhancement Model (PBEM)

1. **Personal Brand Audit**

   - Conduct a comprehensive assessment of your current personal brand.

   - Use methods like SWOT analysis (Strengths, Weaknesses, Opportunities, Threats) to identify areas for growth and opportunities.

2. **Vision and Goal Setting**

   - Establish long-term goals for your professional development and personal brand.

   - Set SMART (specific, measurable, attainable, relevant, and time-bound) objectives.

3. **Strategic Skill Acquisition**

   - Identify key skills and knowledge areas needed to achieve your goals.

   - Prioritise skills based on importance and urgency, creating a blueprint for your learning journey.

4. Leveraging Learning Ecosystems

- Engage in various learning environments, including MOOCs (Massive Open Online Course), webinars, podcasts, and formal education programmes.

- Benefit from both formal and informal learning opportunities.

5. Interactive Learning Communities

- Participate in online and offline learning communities.

- Engage in professional associations, forums, and discussion groups to access diverse perspectives and enhance your learning experience.

6. Personal Learning Network (PLN)

- Connect with mentors, thought leaders and industry experts to build a Personal Learning Network (PLN).

- Use social media platforms to follow and engage with industry experts.

7. Action-Learning Projects

- Apply newly acquired knowledge and skills through action-learning projects.

- Track your progress and evaluate the outcomes to assess your development.

8. Thought Leadership and Knowledge Sharing

- Share your experiences and learnings with your network.

- Establish yourself as a thought leader by consistently posting insightful content.

9. Iteration and Feedback

- Regularly seek feedback from colleagues, mentors, and your professional network.

- Continuously iterate your learning plan based on new insights and feedback.

10. Holistic Personal Development

- Focus on holistic personal development, including physical and emotional well-being.

- Engage in activities that promote overall well-being, such as mindfulness, exercise, and hobbies.

Applying PBEM to Develop Your Personal Brand

1. Evaluate Your Personal Brand

- Use online tools and surveys to gather feedback on your current brand.

- Identify areas for improvement and strengths to leverage.

2. Define Your Objectives and Vision

- Document your long-term vision and break it into manageable goals.

- Use frameworks like OKRs (Objectives and Key Results) to stay focused.

3. Develop a Strategic Acquisition Plan

- Create a plan for acquiring new skills with deadlines and milestones.

- Utilise resources like books, certifications, and online courses.

4. Engage in Ecosystem Learning

- Enrol in MOOCs, listen to industry podcasts, and attend webinars.
- Participate actively in group projects and discussions.

5. Join Learning Communities

- Seek and join relevant online forums, social media groups, and professional associations.
- Initiate discussions and share knowledge to expand your network.

6. Build Your Personal Learning Network (PLN)

- Identify and connect with industry influencers for mentorship.
- Maintain meaningful relationships through regular communication.

7. Carry Out Action-Learning Projects

- Identify projects where you can apply new skills.
- Track progress and document results to showcase your development.

8. Disseminate Information and Create Thought Leadership

- Share your insights regularly through blogs, videos, or webinars.
- Engage with your audience to increase visibility and credibility.

9. Seek Ongoing Input

- Schedule regular feedback sessions with peers and mentors.

- Use feedback to refine your learning approach and personal brand.

10. Prioritise Holistic Growth

- Allocate time for activities that promote well-being.

- Balance personal and professional goals for long-term success.

By adhering to the Personal Brand Enhancement Model (PBEM), you can systematically improve your knowledge, skills, and professional network, ensuring that you remain competitive, adaptable, and prepared for the ever-changing demands of your industry.

In the next chapter, we will explore the concept of resiliency and how it can enhance your personal brand. Through practical strategies and real-life examples, you will learn how to maintain and strengthen your personal brand amidst challenges and setbacks.

Chapter 8

Strategy 8 - Resiliency: Maintaining your Personal Brand Amidst Trials

"Resilience is not about overcoming; it's about becoming." – Sherri Mandell

Opening Story: Amit's Journey of Resilience

Amit, a seasoned operations manager in Mumbai, had always prided himself on his problem-solving skills and ability to manage complex projects. However, when his company underwent a significant restructuring, Amit found himself facing unexpected challenges. The restructuring led to a reduction in staff, increased workload, and uncertainty about the future. For the first time in his career, Amit felt overwhelmed and unsure of how to navigate the turbulent waters.

Determined to maintain his personal brand and rise above the challenges, Amit decided to focus on building resilience. He started by seeking support from mentors and colleagues, adopting stress management techniques, and setting realistic goals. Amit also invested time in professional development to enhance his skills and adapt to the new organisational structure. Through perseverance and a resilient mindset, Amit not only managed to navigate the restructuring but also emerged as a stronger leader. His ability to maintain composure and continue delivering results earned him recognition and respect from his peers and superiors.

The Importance of Resiliency in Personal Branding

Resiliency is the ability to bounce back from adversity and adapt to change. In the context of personal branding, resiliency is crucial for maintaining and strengthening your brand amidst challenges and setbacks. Whether facing professional setbacks, personal challenges, or industry disruptions, resilience allows you to navigate difficulties while preserving your personal brand's integrity and credibility.

A resilient personal brand demonstrates your ability to handle adversity, learn from experiences, and continue growing. It shows that you can remain composed under pressure, adapt to changing circumstances, and emerge stronger from challenges. Building resilience not only enhances your personal brand but also makes you a more effective and trusted leader.

Key benefits of resiliency in personal branding include:

- **Sustaining Credibility**: Maintaining your credibility and reputation even during challenging times.

- **Enhancing Adaptability**: Demonstrating your ability to adapt to change and remain effective in various situations.

- **Building Trust**: Earning the trust and respect of colleagues, employers, and clients through your resilience.

- **Fostering Growth**: Using setbacks as opportunities for learning and growth, strengthening your personal brand over time.

The Process of Building Resiliency

Building resilience involves developing strategies and habits that enable you to navigate challenges and setbacks effectively. Here's a detailed guide to help you cultivate resilience in your personal and professional life:

1. **Develop a Positive Mindset**

   - Cultivate a positive mindset by focusing on your strengths and achievements. Remind yourself of past successes and how you have overcome challenges.

   - Practice gratitude and mindfulness to maintain a positive outlook. Reflect on the things you are grateful for and stay present in the moment.

2. **Set Realistic Goals**

   - Set realistic and achievable goals that align with your personal and professional aspirations. Break larger goals into smaller, manageable steps.

   - Regularly review and adjust your goals to reflect changing circumstances and priorities.

3. **Seek Support and Build a Network**

   - Build a strong support network of mentors, colleagues, friends, and family. Seek their guidance, feedback, and encouragement during challenging times.

   - Join professional associations and networking groups to connect with peers who can offer support and share experiences.

4. Enhance Stress Management Skills

- Develop effective stress management techniques, such as deep breathing exercises, meditation, and physical activity. Incorporate these practices into your daily routine.

- Identify stressors and create strategies to manage them. Practice time management and prioritise tasks to reduce stress.

5. Embrace Adaptability

- Cultivate adaptability by being open to change and willing to learn new skills. View challenges as opportunities for growth and innovation.

- Stay informed about industry trends and developments to anticipate and prepare for changes.

6. Reflect and Learn from Experiences

- Regularly reflect on your experiences and identify key takeaways. Consider what you have learned from challenges and how you can apply these lessons in the future.

- Use setbacks as opportunities for growth and development. Embrace a growth mindset and view failures as valuable learning experiences.

7. Maintain a Healthy Work-Life Balance

- Prioritise self-care and maintain a healthy work-life balance. Ensure you allocate time for relaxation, hobbies, and spending time with loved ones.

- Set boundaries to prevent burnout and maintain your overall well-being.

8. Stay Committed to Your Values

- Stay true to your core values and principles, even during challenging times. Let your values guide your decisions and actions.

- Communicate your values consistently through your personal brand to build trust and credibility.

Real-World Corporate Examples of Resiliency

Case Study 1

Rahul Jain, Suparshva Swabs

Background

- **Role**: Second-generation entrepreneur at Suparshva Swabs

- **Initial Product**: Personal hygiene products like cotton buds

Resiliency in Action

- **Pandemic Challenge**: During the COVID-19 pandemic, there was a sudden and massive demand for polyester swabs essential for testing.

- **Adaptation**: Rahul Jain demonstrated remarkable resilience and leadership by swiftly pivoting the company's production lines from 100% cotton to polyester-spun swabs within just ten days. This involved re-engineering existing machinery, training staff on new production processes, and ensuring quality control in a very short timeframe.

- **Outcome**: This rapid transformation enabled Suparshva Swabs to meet national demands effectively, positioning the company as a crucial supplier during the crisis. Their ability to adapt quickly not only helped in fulfilling the urgent needs but also ensured the company's operational continuity and relevance in a critical market.

Building a Strong Personal Brand

- **Attributes**: Rahul's actions during this period highlighted his innovation, quick decision-making, and strong leadership in times of crisis. His ability to steer the company through unprecedented challenges showcased his resilience and adaptability.

- **Impact**: His leadership significantly strengthened his personal brand as a resilient and forward-thinking leader, enhancing his reputation both within and outside the industry. The success in adapting to the pandemic's demands also underscored Suparshva Swabs' capability to respond effectively under pressure, further elevating the company's brand.

Case Study 2

Puneet Chhatwal, IHCL (Indian Hotels Company Limited)

Background

- **Role**: MD and CEO of IHCL

- **Industry Challenge**: The hospitality industry was severely impacted by COVID-19 lockdowns and travel restrictions, leading to a sharp decline in business.

Resiliency in Action

- **Innovation**: Puneet Chhatwal led the launch of Qmin, a food delivery service, in just six weeks to mitigate the impact of the lockdowns. This rapid deployment involved leveraging IHCL's culinary expertise, integrating digital platforms for seamless customer interaction, and establishing a robust logistics network to ensure timely deliveries.

- **Engagement**: Maintained engagement with customers through digital and social media channels, providing personalised orders, curated menus, and real-time delivery tracking through the Qmin app. This initiative not only catered to existing customers but also attracted new ones by offering high-quality dining experiences at home.

- **Outcome**: The Qmin initiative kept the company connected with its customers, maintained brand visibility, and expanded service offerings despite the challenging circumstances. It also provided an alternative revenue stream, helping IHCL navigate through the financial pressures of the pandemic.

Building a Strong Personal Brand

- **Attributes**: Puneet Chhatwal's quick, innovative response to the crisis, focus on customer-centric solutions, and strategic foresight were pivotal. His actions highlighted his ability to adapt to new challenges and maintain customer engagement under difficult conditions.

- **Impact**: This move reinforced his personal brand as a resilient and customer-focused leader, ensuring the company's survival and growth during tough times. His leadership during the crisis showcased his capability to innovate and adapt, enhancing his reputation as a dynamic leader in the hospitality industry.

These examples illustrate how resilience, coupled with strategic thinking and quick adaptation, can significantly enhance one's personal brand, particularly in the corporate world.

Leveraging Resiliency for Career Advancement

Resiliency plays a crucial role in career advancement. By demonstrating your ability to navigate challenges and adapt to change, you can enhance your personal brand, increase your value to employers, and achieve your career goals.

1. **Maintaining Credibility During Setbacks**

    *   During challenging times, maintaining your credibility is essential. Stay true to your values, communicate transparently, and uphold your commitments.

    *   Demonstrate integrity and professionalism in your actions and decisions. Your ability to maintain credibility will earn you the trust and respect of colleagues, employers, and clients.

2. **Adapting to Changing Circumstances**

    *   The professional landscape is constantly evolving, with new technologies, regulations, and market conditions emerging regularly. Resilience enables you to adapt to these changes and remain effective in your role.

    *   Stay informed about industry trends and developments. Seek out opportunities to learn new skills and enhance your adaptability.

3. Building Trust Through Resilient Leadership

- Resilient leaders inspire trust and confidence in their teams. By demonstrating your ability to navigate challenges and support your team, you can build strong relationships and foster a positive work environment.

- Communicate openly with your team, provide support during difficult times, and lead by example. Your resilient leadership will enhance your personal brand and contribute to your team's success.

4. Using Setbacks as Opportunities for Growth

- View setbacks as opportunities for learning and growth. Reflect on your experiences, identify key takeaways, and apply these lessons to future challenges.

- Embrace a growth mindset and view failures as valuable learning experiences. Use setbacks to develop new skills and strategies for success.

5. Enhancing Your Problem-Solving Skills

- Resilience enhances your problem-solving skills by enabling you to remain calm and focused under pressure. Use challenges as opportunities to develop innovative solutions and demonstrate your value to employers.

- Approach problems with a positive mindset and a willingness to explore new approaches. Your ability to solve problems effectively will enhance your personal brand and career prospects.

Networking and Resiliency: A Synergistic Relationship

Networking and resiliency are closely related and can mutually reinforce each other. By combining networking with resiliency, you can maximise your personal and professional growth.

1. **Leveraging Your Network for Support**

   - Use your professional network to seek support during challenging times. Reach out to mentors, colleagues, and peers for guidance, feedback, and encouragement.

   - Join professional associations and networking groups to connect with individuals who can offer support and share experiences.

2. **Building Resilient Relationships**

   - Build resilient relationships by being supportive and reliable. Offer assistance and encouragement to your network during their challenging times.

   - Foster strong connections by demonstrating your resilience and adaptability. Your ability to maintain strong relationships will enhance your personal brand.

3. **Engaging in Collaborative Problem-Solving**

   - Engage in collaborative problem-solving with your network. Seek input and ideas from diverse perspectives to develop innovative solutions to challenges.

   - Use collaborative efforts to build trust and strengthen relationships within your network.

4. **Sharing Resiliency Strategies**

   - Share your resiliency strategies and experiences with your network. Provide insights and tips on how to navigate challenges and build resilience.

   - Engage in discussions and workshops on resiliency to learn from others and enhance your strategies.

5. **Building a Supportive Community**

   - Create a supportive community that fosters resilience and growth. Encourage open communication, collaboration, and mutual support within your network.

   - Use your community to share resources, insights, and opportunities for learning and development.

Introducing the Resilient Branding Integration Model (RBIM)

The Resilient Branding Integration Model (RBIM) provides a structured approach to integrating resilience into your personal brand. This model focuses on blending resilience-building strategies with personal branding to create a robust and enduring professional presence.

Components of the Resilient Branding Integration Model (RBIM)

1. **Embrace a Growth Mindset**

   - **Cultivate Growth-Oriented Thinking**: Embrace the belief that your abilities and intelligence can be developed with effort, learning, and persistence. A growth mindset will help you view challenges as opportunities for development rather than threats.

- **Celebrate Progress**: Focus on the progress you make, no matter how small. Celebrate your successes and learn from your setbacks.

2. Develop Emotional Intelligence

- **Enhance Self-Awareness**: Understand your emotions, strengths, and weaknesses. Regularly reflect on your emotional responses to different situations and how they impact your behaviour and decisions.

- **Practice Empathy**: Develop the ability to understand and share the feelings of others. Empathy strengthens your relationships and helps you build a supportive network.

3. Foster a Culture of Continuous Improvement

- **Commit to Lifelong Learning**: Continuously seek knowledge and skills that enhance your professional capabilities. Engage in formal education, online courses, and self-directed learning.

- **Implement Feedback Loops**: Actively seek feedback from mentors, colleagues, and peers. Use this feedback to identify areas for improvement and make necessary adjustments.

4. Build Mental Agility

- **Adapt to Change Quickly**: Cultivate the ability to adjust your thinking and strategies in response to changing circumstances. Stay flexible and open-minded.

- **Practice Problem-Solving**: Enhance your problem-solving skills by tackling complex issues and finding creative solutions. Engage in activities that challenge your cognitive abilities.

5. **Establish Resilient Communication**

- **Communicate Transparently**: Maintain open and honest communication with your network. Share your experiences, both positive and negative, to build trust and authenticity.

- **Listen Actively**: Develop active listening skills to understand others' perspectives fully. This helps in building strong, supportive relationships.

6. **Promote Physical and Mental Well-being**

- **Engage in Regular Exercise**: Physical activity boosts your mental and emotional health. Incorporate regular exercise into your routine to maintain energy and reduce stress.

- **Practice Mindfulness and Relaxation Techniques**: Use mindfulness practices, such as meditation and deep breathing, to stay present and manage stress effectively.

7. **Create a Supportive Environment**

- **Build a Network of Allies**: Surround yourself with supportive and like-minded individuals who encourage your growth. Engage in networking groups and professional associations.

- **Provide Support to Others**: Offer your support and assistance to colleagues and peers. Building a culture of mutual support enhances overall resilience.

8. Strengthen Decision-Making Skills

- **Develop Decisiveness**: Enhance your ability to make informed decisions quickly. Practice making decisions under pressure to build confidence.

- **Reflect on Outcomes**: After making decisions, reflect on the outcomes and learn from them. This helps in refining your decision-making process over time.

9. Enhance Technological Proficiency

- **Stay Updated with Technology**: Continuously update your skills in using relevant technologies. Embrace digital tools that can enhance your productivity and efficiency.

- **Leverage Online Communities**: Engage with online communities and forums related to your field. Use these platforms to share knowledge and gain insights from others.

10. Promote Ethical Integrity

- **Adhere to Ethical Standards**: Maintain high ethical standards in all your professional dealings. Integrity builds trust and strengthens your personal brand.

- **Advocate for Ethical Practices**: Promote ethical practices within your organisation and network. Lead by example and inspire others to uphold similar values.

Applying the RBIM Model

To effectively apply the RBIM model, follow these steps:

1. **Assess Your Current Practices**: Evaluate your current strategies for building resilience and personal branding. Identify areas where you can integrate the RBIM components.

2. **Set Specific Goals**: Based on your assessment, set specific goals for implementing the RBIM components. Create a detailed plan outlining the steps you will take.

3. **Monitor Your Progress**: Regularly review your progress towards achieving your goals. Adjust your strategies as needed to stay on track.

4. **Reflect and Adapt**: Continuously reflect on your experiences and the effectiveness of your strategies. Be willing to adapt and refine your approach to achieve better results.

5. **Engage with Your Network**: Actively engage with your professional network to share your journey and gain support. Collaborate with others to enhance your learning and growth.

By adopting the Resilient Branding Integration Model, you can build a strong personal brand that is resilient, adaptable, and enduring. This model provides a comprehensive framework for integrating resilience into your personal and professional development, ensuring long-term success and fulfilment.

Conclusion: The Power of Resiliency

Resiliency is essential for maintaining and strengthening your personal brand amidst challenges and setbacks. By cultivating resilience, you can navigate difficulties, adapt to change, and continue growing. Embrace the power of resiliency and let it guide you towards personal and professional success.

In the next chapter, we will explore the concept of reinvention and how it can enhance your personal brand. Through practical strategies and real-life examples, you will learn how to reinvent yourself and stay relevant in a dynamic professional landscape.

Chapter 9

Strategy 9 - Reinvention: Knowing When and How to Pivot Your Personal Brand

"Every success story is a tale of constant adaptation, revision, and change." – Richard Branson

Opening Story: Shweta's Career Reinvention

Shweta, a marketing professional in Mumbai, had built a solid career in traditional marketing over the past decade. However, as the digital landscape evolved, Shweta noticed a significant shift in her industry. The demand for digital marketing expertise was growing rapidly, and traditional marketing strategies were becoming less effective. Shweta realised that to stay relevant and competitive, she needed to reinvent her personal brand.

Determined to pivot her career, Shweta began by upskilling herself in digital marketing. She enrolled in online courses, attended industry conferences, and sought mentorship from digital marketing experts. Shweta also started a blog to share her insights and experiences, building an online presence that showcased her new skills and expertise. Over time, her efforts paid off. Shweta successfully transitioned into a digital marketing role, and her personal brand as a forward-thinking, adaptable professional was solidified. Her story of reinvention not only enhanced her career but also inspired others to embrace change and stay relevant in their fields.

The Importance of Reinvention in Personal Branding

Reinvention is the process of transforming or pivoting your personal brand to stay relevant, competitive, and aligned with your evolving goals and industry trends. In today's dynamic professional landscape, the ability to reinvent yourself is crucial for sustained success. Whether due to industry changes, personal growth, or shifting career aspirations, reinvention allows you to adapt and thrive in new environments.

A successful reinvention involves more than just acquiring new skills; it requires a strategic approach to redefining your personal brand. It involves understanding the current market demands, identifying your strengths and areas for growth, and effectively communicating your new value proposition to your audience.

Key benefits of reinvention in personal branding include:

- **Staying Relevant**: Adapting to industry changes and market demands to remain competitive.

- **Enhancing Expertise**: Expanding your knowledge and skills to enter new roles or industries.

- **Demonstrating Flexibility**: Showcasing your ability to adapt and thrive in changing environments.

- **Achieving Career Growth**: Opening doors to new opportunities and career advancements.

The Process of Reinventing Your Personal Brand

Reinventing your personal brand involves several steps. Here's a detailed guide to help you navigate the process effectively:

1. **Assess Your Current Brand and Goals**

   - Start by assessing your current personal brand and identifying areas that need change. Reflect on your strengths, skills, and achievements, as well as areas for growth.

   - Define your goals for reinvention. Consider why you want to reinvent your brand and what you hope to achieve. Set specific, measurable, achievable, relevant, and time-bound (SMART) goals.

2. **Research Industry Trends and Opportunities**

   - Conduct thorough research to understand current industry trends, market demands, and emerging opportunities. Identify skills and expertise that are in high demand.

   - Analyse how these trends align with your strengths and interests. Look for gaps that you can fill with your unique skills and experiences.

3. **Identify Skills and Knowledge Gaps**

   - Identify the skills and knowledge you need to acquire to successfully pivot your brand. Consider both technical skills and soft skills that are relevant to your new direction.

   - Create a learning plan to address these gaps. This may include formal education, online courses, certifications, workshops, and self-study.

4. Build a New Value Proposition

- Develop a new value proposition that reflects your reinvented brand. Clearly articulate the unique value you bring to your new role or industry.

- Craft a compelling narrative that highlights your journey of reinvention and how your new skills and expertise address the needs of your target audience.

5. Update Your Online Presence

- Revamp your online presence to reflect your reinvented brand. Update your LinkedIn profile, personal website, and social media profiles with your new value proposition, skills, and achievements.

- Share content that showcases your new expertise. This could include blog posts, articles, videos, and case studies that highlight your journey and insights.

6. Engage with Your Network

- Communicate your reinvention to your professional network. Share your new direction and value proposition with colleagues, mentors, and industry peers.

- Seek feedback and support from your network. Engage in discussions, attend industry events, and participate in online communities to build relationships and enhance your visibility.

7. Demonstrate Your New Expertise

- Look for opportunities to demonstrate your new skills and knowledge. This could include taking on new projects, participating in industry panels, and speaking at conferences.

- Share success stories and case studies that highlight the impact of your new expertise. Use these examples to build credibility and reinforce your reinvented brand.

8. Continuously Monitor and Adjust

- Regularly review your progress and adjust your strategy as needed. Monitor industry trends, seek feedback, and be open to further adjustments.

- Stay committed to continuous learning and growth. Reinvention is an ongoing process that requires adaptability and a willingness to evolve.

Real-World Corporate Examples of Reinvention

Case Study 1: Aditya Ghosh

Background

- **Role**: Former President of IndiGo Airlines, current CEO of India and South Asia at OYO Rooms

- **Initial Career**: Legal professional with no prior experience in aviation

Reinvention in Action

- **Transition to Aviation**: I joined IndiGo in 2008 with no aviation experience, and I am rapidly learning the industry and its complexities.

- **Leadership Success**: Under his leadership, IndiGo grew to become the largest and most profitable airline in India.

- **Further Reinvention**: After leaving IndiGo, he joined OYO Rooms, leading the company as CEO for India and South

Asia, demonstrating his ability to adapt to new sectors and roles.

Building a Strong Personal Brand

- **Attributes**: Continuous learning, adaptability, and strategic vision.

- **Impact**: His successful transitions across different industries underscore his commitment to reinvention and lifelong learning, strengthening his personal brand as a versatile and dynamic leader.

Case Study 2: Vineet Nayar

Background

- **Role**: Former CEO of HCL Technologies

- **Initial Career**: Various roles within HCL before rising to CEO

Reinvention in Action

- **Transformative Leadership**: As CEO, Nayar implemented the "Employees First, Customers Second" philosophy, radically changing the company's culture and operations.

- **Innovative Strategies**: Focused on empowering employees, fostering innovation, and improving customer satisfaction, leading to significant growth and global recognition for HCL.

- **Post-HCL Ventures**: After HCL, he founded the Sampark Foundation, focusing on improving education in India and showcasing his ability to apply his leadership skills to new domains.

Building a Strong Personal Brand:

- **Attributes**: Visionary leadership, innovation, and social impact.

- **Impact**: His ability to reinvent himself and apply his skills to different sectors has enhanced his personal brand as a transformative leader and social entrepreneur.

These examples illustrate the importance of reinvention in one's professional journey and being ready to explore new challenges in building and maintaining a strong personal brand. By continuously exploring and taking up new challenges and embracing changes, professionals can navigate various industries and roles, enhancing their influence and reputation in the corporate world.

Practical Exercises for Reinventing Your Personal Brand

To help you effectively reinvent your personal brand, here are some practical exercises:

1. The Brand Assessment Exercise

- Assess your current personal brand by reflecting on your strengths, skills, and achievements. Identify areas that need change and opportunities for growth.

- Define your goals for reinvention and set specific, measurable, achievable, relevant, and time-bound (SMART) goals.

2. The Industry Research Exercise

- Conduct thorough research to understand current industry trends, market demands, and emerging opportunities. Identify skills and expertise that are in high demand.

- Analyse how these trends align with your strengths and interests. Look for gaps that you can fill with your unique skills and experiences.

3. The Skills Gap Analysis

- Identify the skills and knowledge you need to acquire to successfully pivot your brand. Consider both technical skills and soft skills that are relevant to your new direction.

- Create a learning plan to address these gaps. This may include formal education, online courses, certifications, workshops, and self-study.

4. The Value Proposition Development

- Develop a new value proposition that reflects your reinvented brand. Clearly articulate the unique value you bring to your new role or industry.

- Craft a compelling narrative that highlights your journey of reinvention and how your new skills and expertise address the needs of your target audience.

5. The Online Presence Revamp

- Revamp your online presence to reflect your reinvented brand. Update your LinkedIn profile, personal website, and social media profiles with your new value proposition, skills, and achievements.

- Share content that showcases your new expertise. This could include blog posts, articles, videos, and case studies that highlight your journey and insights.

6. The Network Engagement Plan

- Communicate your reinvention to your professional network. Share your new direction and value proposition with colleagues, mentors, and industry peers.

- Seek feedback and support from your network. Engage in discussions, attend industry events, and participate in online communities to build relationships and enhance your visibility.

7. The Expertise Demonstration Exercise

- Look for opportunities to demonstrate your new skills and knowledge. This could include taking on new projects, participating in industry panels, and speaking at conferences.

- Share success stories and case studies that highlight the impact of your new expertise. Use these examples to build credibility and reinforce your reinvented brand.

8. The Continuous Monitoring and Adjustment Plan

- Regularly review your progress and adjust your strategy as needed. Monitor industry trends, seek feedback, and be open to further adjustments.

- Stay committed to continuous learning and growth. Reinvention is an ongoing process that requires adaptability and a willingness to evolve.

Leveraging Digital Tools for Reinvention

Several digital tools can support your efforts to reinvent your personal brand. Here are some recommended tools:

1. LinkedIn

- LinkedIn is a premier platform for professional networking and personal branding. Use LinkedIn to showcase your new skills, share content, and connect with industry peers.

- Join LinkedIn groups related to your new direction and participate in discussions to enhance your visibility.

2. Coursera

- Coursera offers a wide range of courses and certifications from top universities and institutions. Use Coursera to acquire new skills and knowledge relevant to your reinvention.

- Complete courses and certifications that align with your goals and add them to your LinkedIn profile.

3. Medium

- Medium is a popular platform for publishing articles and blog posts. Use Medium to share your insights and experiences related to your reinvention.

- Engage with the Medium community by reading, clapping for, and commenting on other writers' articles.

4. YouTube

- YouTube is an excellent platform for sharing video content. Create a YouTube channel to share educational videos, tutorials, and insights related to your new expertise.

- Use storytelling techniques to make your videos engaging and relatable. Promote your videos on your social media platforms and website.

5. WordPress

- WordPress is a versatile platform for creating a personal website or blog. Use WordPress to showcase your portfolio, share your achievements, and provide examples of your work.

- Optimise your website for search engines (SEO) to increase its visibility and attract relevant visitors.

6. Hootsuite

- Hootsuite is a social media management tool that allows you to schedule and manage your social media posts across multiple platforms. Use Hootsuite to streamline your social media efforts and ensure consistent engagement with your audience.

7. Google Analytics

- Google Analytics is a powerful tool for tracking and measuring website performance. Use Google Analytics to monitor your website traffic, user behaviour, and content performance.

- Use these insights to refine your strategy and continuously improve your online presence.

Networking and Reinvention: A Synergistic Relationship

Networking and reinvention are closely related and can mutually reinforce each other. By combining networking with reinvention, you can maximise your personal and professional growth.

1. **Leveraging Your Network for Reinvention**

   - Use your professional network to seek support and guidance during your reinvention. Reach out to mentors, colleagues, and peers for feedback and encouragement.

   - Join professional associations and networking groups related to your new direction to connect with individuals who can offer support and share experiences.

2. **Building New Relationships**

   - Build new relationships with industry peers and experts in your new field. Engage in discussions, attend industry events, and participate in online communities to build connections.

   - Use your new relationships to gain insights, share experiences, and enhance your visibility in your new direction.

3. **Sharing Your Reinvention Journey**

   - Share your reinvention journey with your network. Post updates on social media, write blog posts and participate in online discussions to showcase your new direction and value proposition.

   - Engage with your network by sharing insights, asking for feedback, and offering support to others who are also undergoing reinvention.

4. **Engaging in Collaborative Learning**

   - Engage in collaborative learning experiences, such as study groups, project teams, and online forums. Collaborating with others can enhance your learning and provide diverse perspectives.

- Use collaborative learning to build relationships and expand your professional network.

5. **Building a Reinvention Ecosystem**

   - Create an ecosystem that integrates reinvention and networking. This includes having a cohesive reinvention plan, actively engaging with your network, and leveraging online platforms.

   - Use tools like LinkedIn Learning and professional associations to access educational resources and connect with industry peers.

Introducing The Reinvention Influence Model (RIM) - A New Approach

Although we discussed a few practical exercises for reinventing personal branding, let's examine these points through a model. The Reinvention Influence Model (RIM) offers a comprehensive framework for systematically reinventing your personal brand. This model emphasises strategic planning, continuous learning, and proactive engagement to ensure successful transformation.

Components of the Reinvention Influence Model (RIM)

1. **Vision Articulation and Goal Setting**

   - **Define Your Vision:**

     - Establish a clear vision for your future career and personal brand. Envision where you want to be in five, ten, or twenty years.

- **SMART Goals:**
  - Set Specific, Measurable, Achievable, Relevant, and Time-bound goals that align with your vision. These goals will guide your reinvention journey.

2. **In-Depth Industry Research**

- **Market Intelligence:**
  - Conduct extensive research on industry trends, market demands, and technological advancements. Utilise industry reports, webinars, and professional forums.

- **Gap Identification:**
  - Identify gaps in the market that align with your strengths and passions. Focus on areas where you can provide unique value.

3. **Strategic Skill Development**

- **Skill Mapping:**
  - Create a comprehensive map of your current skills and areas for development. Prioritise skills that will have the most significant impact on your career.

- **Learning Roadmap:**
  - Develop a personalised learning roadmap that includes formal education, certifications, online courses, and self-study. Commit to continuous learning.

4. **Dynamic Value Proposition Crafting**

- **Value Proposition Statement:**
  - Craft a dynamic value proposition that evolves with your growth. Clearly articulate how your new skills and expertise provide unique value.

- **Storytelling:**
  - Use storytelling techniques to highlight your journey and the transformation of your brand. Share your experiences and insights with your audience.

5. **Enhanced Online Presence**

- **Profile Optimisation:**
  - Optimise your online profiles to reflect your reinvented brand. Regularly update your LinkedIn, personal website, and other professional platforms.

- **Content Strategy:**
  - Develop a robust content strategy that includes blogs, videos, and social media posts. Share insights, case studies, and thought leadership pieces.

6. **Mentorship and Coaching Integration**

- **Structured Mentorship:**
  - Integrate mentorship and coaching into your reinvention strategy. Seek regular feedback and guidance from mentors.

- **Professional Development Groups:**
  - Join professional development groups and networks to connect with peers and mentors who can support your journey.

7. **Collaborative Projects and Innovation Challenges**

- **Participation in Projects:**
  - Engage in collaborative projects, hackathons, and innovation challenges. Use these opportunities to demonstrate your new skills.

- **Portfolio Building:**
  - Build a portfolio of work that showcases your expertise and adaptability. Highlight your contributions and achievements in these projects.

8. **Thought Leadership Establishment**

- **Industry Contributions:**
  - Position yourself as a thought leader by contributing to industry publications, speaking at conferences, and hosting webinars.

- Content **Creation**:
  - Share your knowledge and insights through blog posts, articles, podcasts, and videos. Build a following by consistently providing valuable content.

9. **Progress Monitoring and Strategic Adjustment**

- **Regular Assessments:**
  - Conduct regular assessments of your progress and strategies. Use feedback to refine your approach and make necessary adjustments.

- **Agility and Adaptability:**
  - Stay flexible and open to changes. Adapt your strategies based on market dynamics and personal growth.

10. **Holistic Personal Development**

- **Balanced Growth:**
  - Focus on holistic development, including physical, mental, and emotional well-being. Engage in activities that promote overall health and happiness.

- **Work-Life Integration:**
  - Ensure a healthy balance between professional goals and personal life. Prioritise self-care and engage in activities that bring joy and relaxation.

Reinvention is not just about acquiring new skills; it's about evolving your entire persona to stay relevant and impactful in a dynamic world. The Reinvention Influence Model (RIM) provides a structured approach to navigating this journey. By continuously learning, adapting, and leveraging your network, you can build a robust personal brand that stands the test of time. Embrace the journey of reinvention with a positive mindset, and let your personal brand reflect your growth, adaptability, and unwavering commitment to excellence.

In the next chapter, we will explore the concept of consistency and how it can enhance your personal brand. Through practical strategies and real-life examples, you will learn how to maintain consistency in your brand message and actions to build trust and credibility.

Chapter 10

Strategy 10 - Consistency: Keeping Your Personal Brand Aligned and Reliable

"Consistency is what transforms average into excellence." – Tony Robbins

Opening Story: Priya's Path to Consistency

Priya, an HR professional in Bangalore, was known for her innovative approaches to employee engagement and organisational development. However, she struggled to establish a consistent personal brand. Priya often found herself overwhelmed with various projects and responsibilities, leading to a fragmented online presence and inconsistent communication. She realised that to build a strong personal brand, she needed to align her actions and messages consistently across all platforms.

Determined to address this, Priya began by defining her core values and key messages. She then developed a content calendar to ensure regular and consistent updates across her social media profiles, blog, and professional network. Priya also created a style guide to maintain a uniform tone and visual identity. Over time, her efforts paid off. Priya's consistent personal brand enhanced her credibility and visibility, making her a sought-after expert in her field. Her story of achieving consistency not only strengthened her personal brand but also demonstrated the power of alignment and reliability.

The Importance of Consistency in Personal Branding

Consistency is the cornerstone of a strong personal brand. It involves aligning your actions, messages, and visual identity across all touchpoints to create a cohesive and reliable image. A consistent personal brand builds trust, credibility, and recognition, making it easier for others to understand who you are, what you stand for, and what value you bring.

In a world where first impressions and perceptions are often formed quickly, consistency helps reinforce your brand identity and ensure that your audience receives a clear and unified message. Whether through social media, professional interactions, or public appearances, maintaining consistency in your personal brand enhances your reputation and makes you more memorable.

Key benefits of consistency in personal branding include:

- **Building Trust**: Consistency builds trust by demonstrating reliability and integrity.

- **Enhancing Credibility**: A consistent brand enhances your credibility and reinforces your expertise.

- **Increasing Recognition**: Consistency makes your brand more recognisable and memorable.

- **Strengthening Relationships**: A consistent brand fosters stronger relationships with your audience and network.

The Process of Maintaining Consistency

Maintaining consistency in your personal brand involves several steps. Here's a detailed guide to help you achieve and sustain alignment in your branding efforts:

1. **Define Your Core Values and Key Messages**

   - Start by defining your core values and the key messages you want to convey through your personal brand. Consider what you stand for, what you believe in, and what value you bring to your audience.

   - Create a value statement and a list of key messages that reflect your brand identity. Ensure these elements are clear, concise, and aligned with your goals.

2. **Develop a Brand Style Guide**

   - Create a brand style guide that outlines the visual and verbal elements of your personal brand. This includes your logo, colour palette, typography, tone of voice, and messaging guidelines.

   - Use the style guide to maintain a uniform look and feel across all your branding materials, including social media profiles, websites, presentations, and marketing collateral.

3. **Create a Content Calendar**

   - Develop a content calendar to plan and schedule your content updates. This helps ensure regular and consistent communication across all platforms.

   - Include a mix of content types, such as blog posts, social media updates, videos, and newsletters, to keep your audience engaged and informed.

4. Align Your Online and Offline Presence

- Ensure that your online presence aligns with your offline presence. Consistency should be maintained across all touchpoints, including social media, professional interactions, public appearances, and networking events.

- Use the same profile picture, bio, and key messages across all your online profiles to create a cohesive and recognisable brand.

5. Monitor and Review Your Brand

- Regularly monitor your brand to ensure consistency. Review your online profiles, content, and interactions to identify any discrepancies or misalignments.

- Seek feedback from trusted colleagues, mentors, and peers to gain insights into how your brand is perceived and make adjustments as needed.

6. Engage with Your Audience

- Actively engage with your audience to build relationships and reinforce your brand. Respond to comments, participate in discussions, and share valuable insights.

- Consistent engagement helps build trust and credibility, making your brand more reliable and approachable.

7. Adapt and Evolve While Maintaining Core Elements

- Stay open to adapting and evolving your brand as needed, while maintaining the core elements that define your identity. This allows you to stay relevant and responsive to changes in your industry or audience preferences.

- Regularly update your content and messaging to reflect new developments, trends, and insights, while ensuring alignment with your core values and key messages.

Practical Exercises for Maintaining Consistency

To help you achieve and sustain consistency in your personal brand, here are some practical exercises:

1. **The Core Values and Key Messages Exercise**

   - Reflect on your core values and the key messages you want to convey through your personal brand. Write down what you stand for, what you believe in, and what value you bring to your audience.

   - Create a value statement and a list of key messages that reflect your brand identity. Ensure these elements are clear, concise, and aligned with your goals.

2. **The Brand Style Guide Development**

   - Create a brand style guide that outlines the visual and verbal elements of your personal brand. This includes your logo, colour palette, typography, tone of voice, and messaging guidelines.

   - Use the style guide to maintain a uniform look and feel across all your branding materials, including social media profiles, websites, presentations, and marketing collateral.

3. **The Content Calendar Planning**

   - Develop a content calendar to plan and schedule your content updates. This helps ensure regular and consistent communication across all platforms.

- Include a mix of content types, such as blog posts, social media updates, videos, and newsletters, to keep your audience engaged and informed.

4. The Online and Offline Alignment Exercise

- Ensure that your online presence aligns with your offline presence. Consistency should be maintained across all touchpoints, including social media, professional interactions, public appearances, and networking events.

- Use the same profile picture, bio, and key messages across all your online profiles to create a cohesive and recognisable brand.

5. The Brand Monitoring and Review

- Regularly monitor your brand to ensure consistency. Review your online profiles, content, and interactions to identify any discrepancies or misalignments.

- Seek feedback from trusted colleagues, mentors, and peers to gain insights into how your brand is perceived and make adjustments as needed.

6. The Audience Engagement Plan

- Actively engage with your audience to build relationships and reinforce your brand. Respond to comments, participate in discussions, and share valuable insights.

- Consistent engagement helps build trust and credibility, making your brand more reliable and approachable.

7. The Adaptation and Evolution Strategy

- Stay open to adapting and evolving your brand as needed, while maintaining the core elements that define your identity. This allows you to stay relevant and responsive to changes in your industry or audience preferences.

- Regularly update your content and messaging to reflect new developments, trends, and insights, while ensuring alignment with your core values and key messages.

Real-Life Example of Consistency in Building Personal Brand

Case Study 1

Gary Vaynerchuk

Background

- **Role**: Entrepreneur, author, and social media personality
- **Initial Career**: Started by transforming his family's wine business through online marketing.

Consistency in Personal Branding

- **Social Media Presence**: Consistently produces content across multiple platforms, sharing insights on entrepreneurship, marketing, and personal development.

- **Books and Speaking Engagements**: Authored multiple bestsellers and speaks at various global conferences, reinforcing his expertise.

- **Adaptation and Innovation**: Continuously adopts new technologies and platforms to stay relevant, such as launching a successful NFT project.

Building a Strong Personal Brand

- **Attributes**: Consistency, adaptability, and authenticity.

- **Impact**: Gary's ongoing efforts in content creation and thought leadership have solidified his brand as a digital marketing guru and motivational figure.

Case Study 2

Brené Brown

Background

- **Role**: Research professor, author, and public speaker

- **Initial Career**: Academic researcher focusing on vulnerability, courage, and empathy.

Consistency in Personal Branding

- **Publications and Talks**: Authored multiple influential books and delivered widely-viewed TED Talks.

- **Media Presence**: Hosts a podcast and features in various media, discussing personal growth and leadership.

- **Educational Initiatives**: Continues to create courses and programmes that teach her research findings to a broader audience.

Building a Strong Personal Brand

- **Attributes**: Consistency in messages, educational focus, and relatable storytelling.

- **Impact**: Brené's consistent dissemination of her research has strengthened her brand as an expert on vulnerability and leadership.

Leveraging Digital Tools for Consistency

Several digital tools can support your efforts to maintain consistency in your personal brand. Here are some recommended tools:

1. Canva

- Canva is a versatile design tool that allows you to create visually consistent branding materials. Use Canva to design social media graphics, presentations, and marketing collateral that align with your brand style guide.

- Utilise Canva's templates and branding features to maintain a uniform look and feel across all your visuals.

2. Hootsuite

- Hootsuite is a social media management tool that allows you to schedule and manage your social media posts across multiple platforms. Use Hootsuite to ensure consistent communication and engagement with your audience.

- Plan and schedule your content in advance to maintain regular updates and consistent messaging.

3. Google Drive

- Google Drive is a cloud storage and collaboration tool that helps you organise and manage your branding materials. Use Google Drive to store your brand style guide, content calendar, and visual assets.

- Share documents with collaborators and ensure everyone has access to the latest versions of your branding materials.

4. Trello

- Trello is a project management tool that helps you organise and track your branding activities. Use Trello to create boards and cards for your content calendar, branding tasks, and engagement plans.

- Collaborate with team members and set deadlines to ensure consistency in your branding efforts.

5. Mailchimp

- Mailchimp is an email marketing tool that helps you create and send consistent email campaigns. Use Mailchimp to design branded email templates, schedule newsletters, and track campaign performance.

- Ensure your email communications align with your brand style guide and key messages.

6. Brand24

- Brand24 is a social media monitoring tool that helps you track your brand's online presence and engagement. Use Brand24 to monitor mentions, comments, and interactions related to your brand.

- Analyse the data to identify any inconsistencies and make adjustments to maintain a cohesive brand identity.

Networking and Consistency: A Synergistic Relationship

Networking and consistency are closely related and can mutually reinforce each other. By combining networking with consistent branding, you can maximise your personal and professional growth.

1. Leveraging Your Network for Consistency

- Use your professional network to gain feedback on your brand consistency. Reach out to mentors, colleagues, and peers for insights into how your brand is perceived.

- Join professional associations and networking groups to connect with individuals who can offer support and share best practices for maintaining consistency.

2. Building Consistent Relationships

- Build consistent relationships by being reliable and trustworthy. Ensure that your actions and communications align with your core values and key messages.

- Foster strong connections by demonstrating consistency in your interactions and engagements.

3. Sharing Consistent Content

- Share consistent content with your network to reinforce your brand identity. Post regular updates, share valuable insights, and engage in discussions that align with your brand messages.

- Use your content to build relationships and enhance your visibility within your network.

4. Engaging in Collaborative Branding

- Engage in collaborative branding efforts with your network. Partner with industry peers and influencers to create joint content, host events, and participate in discussions.

- Collaborative branding can enhance your credibility and expand your reach while maintaining consistency in your messaging.

5. Building a Consistency Ecosystem

- Create an ecosystem that integrates consistency and networking. This includes having a cohesive brand identity, actively engaging with your network, and leveraging digital tools.

- Use tools like Hootsuite and Trello to manage your branding activities and ensure consistent communication and engagement.

Introducing The Strategic Consistency Framework (SCF)

Introducing a fresh approach to maintaining consistency in your personal brand, the Strategic Consistency Framework (SCF) provides a comprehensive guide to ensure your brand remains cohesive and trustworthy over time. This model emphasises long-term strategies and integrates continuous feedback mechanisms to maintain brand integrity and alignment with personal and professional goals.

Components of the Strategic Consistency Framework (SCF)

1. Establish Core Values and Brand Identity

- Reflect on your personal and professional values and how they align with your goals. Write down your core values and the key messages you want your brand to convey.

- Develop a personal brand identity that reflects these values. Ensure your brand narrative is authentic and resonates with your audience.

2. Craft a Comprehensive Brand Manual

- Develop a detailed brand manual that includes guidelines on visual and verbal elements, such as logos, colour schemes, typography, and tone of voice.

- Use this manual to maintain consistency across all platforms and materials, from social media profiles to presentations and marketing collateral.

3. Implement a Robust Content Strategy

- Create a strategic content plan that outlines the types of content you will produce and how often. This should include blog posts, social media updates, newsletters, videos, and more.

- Use tools like content calendars to schedule and manage your content, ensuring a steady stream of valuable information for your audience.

4. Synchronise Online and Offline Branding

- Ensure that your online persona is a true reflection of your offline activities and vice versa. Use consistent images, bios, and messaging across all platforms.

- Regularly update your profiles to reflect new achievements and milestones, maintaining a cohesive brand image.

5. Continuous Brand Monitoring and Analytics

- Regularly monitor your brand's performance using analytics tools to track engagement, reach, and audience feedback.

- Conduct periodic brand audits to ensure alignment with your core values and goals. Adjust strategies based on insights and feedback.

6. Audience Engagement and Interaction

- Develop an engagement plan to interact consistently with your audience. Respond to comments, participate in relevant discussions, and provide valuable insights.

- Building a community around your brand fosters trust and loyalty, reinforcing your brand's reliability.

7. Adaptability with Core Integrity

- While staying true to your core values, remain adaptable to industry changes and trends. Update your content and strategies to stay relevant.

- Embrace new platforms and technologies to reach a broader audience without compromising your brand's essence.

8. Integrate Feedback and Iterative Improvement

- Actively seek feedback from your audience, peers, and mentors. Use this feedback to refine your brand and address any inconsistencies.

- Implement an iterative process for continuous improvement, ensuring your brand evolves while maintaining its core identity.

9. Foster Collaborative Relationships

- Engage in collaborative projects and partnerships that align with your brand values. These collaborations can enhance your brand's credibility and extend its reach.

- Share insights and learnings from these collaborations to provide added value to your audience.

10. Consistent Content Creation and Sharing

- Commit to a regular schedule of content creation that aligns with your brand's themes and values. This includes articles, case studies, videos, and social media posts.

- Ensure all content is high-quality and reflects your brand's voice and message consistently.

11. Transparent Communication

- Practice transparency in all your communications. Be open about your successes, challenges, and the journey of your brand.

- Transparency builds trust and strengthens the connection with your audience, making your brand more relatable and credible.

12. Strategic Networking

- Leverage your network to maintain and enhance your brand consistency. Engage with industry leaders, join professional groups, and participate in relevant events.

- Use networking opportunities to reinforce your brand message and expand your influence.

13. Document Your Journey

- Maintain a journal or blog documenting your brand's journey, including milestones, challenges, and learnings.

- Sharing this journey with your audience can humanise your brand and provide valuable insights into your growth and resilience.

14. Establish Long-term Brand Goals

- Set long-term goals for your personal brand and create a roadmap to achieve them. These goals should be ambitious yet attainable and aligned with your core values.

- Regularly review and adjust your goals to stay aligned with your evolving personal and professional aspirations.

By adopting the **Strategic Consistency Framework (SCF)**, you can ensure your personal brand remains cohesive, authentic, and adaptable. This approach not only helps in maintaining a strong and reliable brand presence but also prepares you to navigate the ever-changing professional landscape with confidence and clarity. Embrace the principles of SCF to build a personal brand that stands the test of time and continually resonates with your audience.

Conclusion: The Power of Consistency

Consistency is essential for maintaining and strengthening your personal brand. By aligning your actions, messages, and visual identity across all touchpoints, you can create a cohesive and reliable image that builds trust, credibility, and recognition. Embrace the power of consistency and let it guide you towards personal and professional success.

In the next chapter, we will explore the future of personal branding and how to stay ahead of emerging trends. Through practical strategies and real-life examples, you will learn how to adapt and innovate to ensure your personal brand remains relevant and impactful in a dynamic professional landscape.

The Future of Personal Branding

"Brand yourself for the career you want, not the job you have" - Dan Schawbel

Opening Story: Arjun's Vision for the Future

Arjun, an executive coach and thought leader based in Delhi, had built a strong personal brand over the years. Known for his expertise in leadership development and his engaging speaking style, Arjun had successfully positioned himself as a go-to expert in his field. However, as the landscape of personal branding evolved with new technologies and trends, Arjun realised the importance of staying ahead to maintain his brand's relevance and impact.

Determined to future-proof his brand, Arjun began exploring emerging trends and technologies that could enhance his personal branding efforts. He embraced digital tools, started experimenting with AI-driven content creation, and engaged in virtual reality (VR) events to reach a global audience. By continuously adapting and innovating, Arjun not only stayed relevant but also set new standards in his industry. His vision for the future of personal branding inspired others to embrace change and leverage new opportunities to enhance their personal brands.

The Future of Personal Branding

The landscape of personal branding is constantly evolving, driven by technological advancements, changing consumer behaviours, and emerging trends. To stay relevant and impactful, it's essential to anticipate these changes and adapt your personal branding strategies accordingly. The future of personal branding will be shaped by several key trends and technologies, including digital transformation, artificial intelligence (AI), augmented reality (AR), and an increased focus on authenticity and social impact.

Understanding these trends and integrating them into your personal branding efforts can help you stay ahead of the curve and ensure your brand remains compelling and relevant.

Key Trends Shaping the Future of Personal Branding

1. Digital Transformation

The digital age is rapidly changing how we build and maintain personal brands. Embracing digital transformation can elevate your brand to new heights.

- **Leverage Digital Platforms**: Use platforms like LinkedIn, Twitter, and Instagram to showcase your expertise, share valuable content, and connect with a broader audience.

- **Multi-Channel Content**: Develop a strategy that includes blog posts, videos, and podcasts tailored to different platforms and audiences.

- **Utilise Digital Tools**: Tools like Canva for design, Hootsuite for scheduling, and Google Analytics for tracking can help maintain consistency and effectiveness.

2. Artificial Intelligence (AI) and Automation

AI and automation are revolutionising personal branding by enhancing efficiency and providing deeper insights.

- **AI-Driven Content Creation**: Utilise AI tools to generate content ideas, draft posts, and manage your editorial calendar.

- **Automated Social Media Management**: Tools like Buffer and Sprout Social can help you maintain a consistent online presence.

- **Data-Driven Insights**: Use analytics tools to understand audience behaviour and preferences, helping you tailor your content effectively.

3. Augmented Reality (AR) and Virtual Reality (VR)

Emerging technologies like AR and VR offer unique ways to engage your audience.

- **Virtual Reality Events**: Host VR workshops and conferences to create immersive experiences.

- **Augmented Reality Content**: Create interactive AR experiences like filters and virtual try-ons to enhance engagement.

- **Immersive Storytelling**: Use AR and VR to make your brand story more engaging and memorable.

4. Authenticity and Personalisation

In an era of information overload, being authentic and personalised is crucial.

- **Be Authentic**: Share genuine stories and experiences to build trust and credibility.

- **Personalised Content**: Tailor your content to meet the specific needs and preferences of your audience.

- **Engage with Your Audience**: Actively participate in conversations, respond to feedback, and foster a sense of community.

5. **Social Impact and Purpose-Driven Branding**

Modern audiences value brands that contribute positively to society.

- **Define Your Purpose**: Clearly articulate your mission and values.

- **Take Action**: Participate in initiatives that align with your values and communicate these efforts to your audience.

- **Communicate Your Impact**: Share updates on your social impact to build credibility and inspire others.

Practical Exercises for Future-Proofing Your Personal Brand

1. **The Continuous Learning Plan**

   - **Identify Trends**: Stay updated with industry developments.

   - **Set Learning Goals**: Allocate time for continuous learning.

2. **The Digital Tools Assessment**

   - **Evaluate Tools**: Identify where digital tools can enhance your efforts.

   - **Experiment and Invest**: Try new technologies to stay ahead.

3. The Online Presence Audit

- **Conduct an Audit**: Ensure consistency across all platforms.
- **Optimise for SEO**: Regularly update and refine your profiles.

4. The Authenticity and Transparency Exercise

- **Reflect on Stories**: Share authentic experiences.
- **Address Feedback**: Foster transparency in communications.

5. The Purpose-Driven Branding Plan

- **Define Purpose**: Integrate your values into your brand mission.
- **Communicate Impact**: Share your social impact efforts.

6. The Data-Driven Strategy

- **Use Insights**: Inform your strategies with data.
- **Track Performance**: Measure and refine your efforts.

7. The Networking and Collaboration Plan

- **Build Relationships**: Network with industry peers and influencers.
- **Collaborate**: Enhance credibility through joint efforts.

The Continuous Journey of Personal Branding

1. Embrace a Growth Mindset

Embracing a growth mindset is fundamental to personal branding. It's about viewing every challenge as an opportunity to learn and grow, rather than as a setback.

- **Continuous Improvement**: Adopt a mindset where challenges are seen as opportunities to improve. Instead of shying away from difficulties, face them head-on, knowing that each challenge you overcome makes you stronger. For instance, if you receive critical feedback, rather than taking it personally, use it as a chance to refine your skills and approach.

- **Learn and Evolve**: Your strategies for personal branding should not be static. Regularly assess your methods and outcomes and be willing to make changes when necessary. Continuous learning could involve taking up new courses, reading the latest industry trends, or attending workshops. Keep your skills updated and your mind open to new ideas.

2. Stay Connected with Your Audience

Building and maintaining a strong personal brand involves staying connected with your audience. This connection fosters loyalty and trust.

- **Engage Regularly**: Interaction with your audience should be a regular activity. This could be through social media posts, newsletters, or even webinars. Regular engagement keeps your audience informed and involved with your brand, fostering a sense of community and loyalty.

- **Listen and Adapt**: Pay attention to the feedback you receive from your audience. Whether it's through comments on your blog, responses on social media, or feedback from networking events, use this information to adapt and refine your strategies. This shows that you value your audience's opinions and are committed to meeting their needs.

3. Adapt to Industry Changes

The landscape of personal branding is ever-changing, and staying relevant means being adaptable to these changes.

- **Stay Informed**: Regularly update yourself with the latest trends and developments in your industry. Subscribe to industry newsletters, follow thought leaders on social media, and attend relevant conferences and webinars. This ensures that your knowledge and skills remain current.

- **Proactively Adapt**: Use the information you gather to proactively adjust your branding strategies. If a new platform or tool becomes popular in your industry, explore how you can incorporate it into your personal branding efforts. Being proactive rather than reactive keeps you ahead of the curve.

4. Leverage New Opportunities

New opportunities for growth and visibility are constantly emerging. Seizing these opportunities can significantly enhance your personal brand.

- **Explore Innovations**: Stay curious and open to trying new technologies and platforms. Whether it's a new social media channel, a digital marketing tool, or an innovative way to present your content, exploring these innovations can give you a competitive edge.

- **Take Risks**: Sometimes, building a strong personal brand requires stepping out of your comfort zone. This could mean speaking at a conference, publishing a controversial opinion piece, or starting a new venture. Calculated risks can pay off by positioning you as a forward-thinking and dynamic professional.

5. Reflect and Evolve

Regular reflection and evolution are crucial for maintaining a robust personal brand. This continuous process ensures that your brand remains relevant and impactful.

- **Regular Reflection**: Periodically take time to reflect on your personal branding journey. Assess your successes and failures, and identify areas for improvement. This could be through personal introspection, seeking feedback from peers, or even professional coaching.

- **Embrace Change**: Be willing to evolve your strategies and approach as needed. The world is constantly changing, and clinging to outdated methods can hinder your growth. Embrace change as a natural and necessary part of your personal branding journey, and use it as an opportunity to continuously refine and enhance your brand.

By embracing these strategies, you can future-proof your personal brand, ensuring it remains strong, relevant, and impactful in the ever-evolving landscape of personal branding.

Conclusion: Embracing the Future of Personal Branding

The future of personal branding is dynamic, driven by technological advancements, changing consumer behaviours, and emerging trends. To stay relevant and impactful, it's essential to anticipate these changes and adapt your personal branding strategies accordingly.

By embracing digital transformation, leveraging AI and automation, exploring AR and VR, fostering authenticity, and aligning your brand with a meaningful purpose, you can future-proof your personal brand and ensure its long-term success.

The journey of personal branding is continuous, requiring ongoing effort, adaptation, and innovation. Embrace a growth mindset, stay connected with your audience, and leverage new opportunities to enhance your brand. Let the strategies and insights outlined in this book guide you toward personal and professional success in a dynamic and ever-evolving landscape.

Conclusion

Summary of Key Learnings from Each Strategy

Strategy 1: Self-Awareness - Finding Your Authentic Identity

- **Importance**: Understanding your core values, passions, strengths, and weaknesses is crucial for building an authentic personal brand.

- **Key Actions**: Engage in introspection, seek feedback, use personality assessments, and conduct a personal SWOT analysis.

- **Outcome**: Align your personal brand with your true self, ensuring authenticity and consistency in your professional presence.

Strategy 2: Differentiation - Standing Out from the Crowd

- **Importance**: Differentiation is essential in a crowded job market to make you visible and memorable.

- **Key Actions**: Identify unique strengths, craft a Unique Value Proposition (UVP), and leverage market needs.

- **Outcome**: Create a niche for yourself, highlight your unique value, and attract opportunities.

Strategy 3: Building a Value Proposition - Creating a Never-Failing Offer

- **Importance**: A compelling value proposition clearly articulates the unique value you bring to your professional environment.

- **Key Actions**: Identify audience needs, highlight strengths, articulate benefits, and test and refine your value proposition.

- **Outcome**: Communicate your unique offerings effectively, making you indispensable in your professional field.

Strategy 4: Storytelling - Making Your Personal Brand Relatable

- **Importance**: Storytelling transforms your personal brand from a collection of achievements into a compelling narrative.

- **Key Actions**: Identify key moments, define your core message, create a narrative arc, and make your story authentic.

- **Outcome**: Engage, inspire, and connect with your audience on a deep emotional level.

Strategy 5: Networking - Expanding Your Personal Brand's Reach

- **Importance**: Networking enhances visibility, provides valuable opportunities, and reinforces your personal brand.

- **Key Actions**: Build and expand your network, engage in meaningful collaboration, and maintain relationships.

- **Outcome**: Enhance your professional credibility and create meaningful connections that support your brand.

Strategy 6: Online Presence - Digitising Your Personal Brand

- **Importance**: A strong online presence is crucial in the digital age to reach a global audience.

- **Key Actions**: Leverage social media platforms, create and share valuable content, and engage with your audience.

- **Outcome**: Increase visibility, build credibility, and connect with a broader audience.

Strategy 7: Continuous Education - Learning as a Lifelong Endeavour

- **Importance**: Continuous learning ensures that you stay relevant and competitive in your field.

- **Key Actions**: Develop a learning plan, stay updated with industry trends, and seek professional development opportunities.

- **Outcome**: Maintain long-term relevance and demonstrate a commitment to growth and improvement.

Strategy 8: Resiliency - Maintaining Your Personal Brand Amidst Trials

- **Importance**: Resiliency helps you navigate challenges and maintain your personal brand during difficult times.

- **Key Actions**: Embrace change, learn from setbacks, and stay adaptable.

- **Outcome**: Build a personal brand that is strong, flexible, and capable of overcoming adversity.

Strategy 9: Reinvention - Knowing When and How to Pivot Your Personal Brand

- **Importance**: Reinvention allows you to stay relevant and seize new opportunities by adapting your personal brand.

- **Key Actions**: Recognise the need for change, plan your reinvention, and execute the pivot effectively.

- **Outcome**: Ensure your personal brand evolves with market demands and continues to thrive.

Strategy 10: Consistency - Keeping Your Personal Brand Aligned and Reliable

- **Importance**: Consistency builds trust and ensures that your personal brand is reliable and recognisable.

- **Key Actions**: Maintain a consistent message, align your actions with your brand values, and regularly review your brand.

- **Outcome**: Establish a strong, dependable personal brand that resonates with your audience.

Call to Action

As we conclude this journey through the strategies of building and enhancing your personal brand, remember that the power to transform your career lies within you. Here are some final steps to take action:

1. **Reflect and Act**: Take the insights and exercises from this book and apply them to your own personal brand journey. Reflect on your unique strengths, craft your value proposition, and start sharing your story.

2. **Engage Continuously**: Personal branding is not a one-time effort but an ongoing process. Stay engaged, seek feedback, and adapt your strategies as you grow in your career.

3. **Leverage Resources**: Utilise the tools, templates, and exercises provided in this book. They are designed to help you build and maintain a strong personal brand.

4. **Network and Collaborate**: Connect with like-minded professionals, seek mentors, and engage in meaningful collaborations. Building a network of support will enhance your brand and open new opportunities.

5. **Commit to Learning**: Embrace lifelong learning. Stay updated with industry trends, seek new knowledge, and continuously improve your skills.

6. **Stay Resilient and Adaptable**: Be prepared to face challenges and adapt to changes. Resiliency and the ability to reinvent yourself are key to sustaining a strong personal brand.

7. **Consistency is Key**: Ensure that your personal brand remains consistent across all platforms and interactions. Trust and reliability are built through consistency.

Take the first step today. Reflect on your personal brand, set your goals, and embark on this exciting journey of personal and professional growth. Your brand is your promise to the world—make it powerful, authentic, and unforgettable.

Thank you for joining me on this journey. I wish you all the best in building a personal brand that not only stands out but also stands the test of time. Start now, and make your mark in the world!

Sources

- https://www.brainyquote.com/

- **Importance of Personal Branding**

    - https://www.forbes.com/sites/forbesbusinesscouncil/2023/03/30/brand-yourself-build-your-future-the-importance-of-personal-branding-for-professional-success/

- **Digital Tools for Personal Branding:** https://personalbrand.com/13-essential-tools-building-personal-brand/

- **Building a Personal Brand Through Online Presence:** https://digitalmarketinginstitute.com/blog/10-steps-to-building-your-personal-brand-on-social-media

- **Harvard Business Review - Articles on personal branding and professional development:** https://hbr.org/

- **Forbes - Insights and trends related to personal branding and digital presence:** https://www.forbes.com/sites/forbescoachescouncil/2023/08/14/building-a-strong-online-presence-the-power-of-a-consistent-and-authentic-personal-brand/

- **Inc. Magazine - Case studies and tips for personal branding:** https://www.inc.com/

- **Myers-Briggs Type Indicator (MBTI):** https://www.myersbriggs.org/my-mbti-personality-type/myers-briggs-overview/

- **StrengthsFinder:** https://www.gallup.com/cliftonstrengths/en/254033/strengthsfinder.aspx

- **SWOT Analysis:** https://www.mindtools.com/amtbj63/swot-analysis

- **360-Degree Feedback:** https://www.qualtrics.com/en-au/experience-management/employee/360-degree-feedback/

- **Differentiation**: https://seths.blog/2004/04/differentiation/

- **Shantanu Narayen (CEO, Adobe)**

  - https://www.adobe.com/about-adobe/leaders/shantanu-narayen.html

- Arundhati Bhattacharya (Former Chairperson, State Bank of India)

  - https://economictimes.indiatimes.com/magazines/panache/arundhati-bhattacharya-turns-author-shares-she-was-once-on-the-verge-of-quitting-her-career/articleshow/88853311.cms?from=mdr

- John Jantsch Quotes - AZQuotes

- https://www.creativelive.com/class/duct-tape-marketing-john-jantsch/lessons/strategy-business-model

- **A.R. Rahman**

  - : https://www.britannica.com/biography/A-R-Rahman

  - : https://www.grammy.com/artists/ar-rahman/6529

- Kiran Mazumdar-Shaw

- - : https://www.biocon.com/about-us/board-of-directors-biocon/kiran-mazumdar-shaw-biocon/
  - : https://www.forbes.com/profile/kiran-mazumdar-shaw/#:~:text=Kiran%20Mazumdar%2DShaw%2C%20one%20of,factory%20in%20Malaysia's%20Johor%20region.
- https://heidicohen.com/seth-godin-7-truths-at-the-heart-of-marketing-how-to-use-them/
- https://financialbrandforum.com/seth-godin/
- **Howard Schultz and Starbucks:** https://stories.starbucks.com/leadership/howard-schultz/
- https://www.forbes.com/profile/howard-schultz/#:~:text=Howard%20Schultz%20took%20charge%20of,stepping%20down%20in%20early%202023.
- **Richard Branson and Virgin Group:** https://www.virgin.com/branson-family/richard-branson
- https://www.britannica.com/money/Richard-Branson
- **Porter Gale - "Your network is your net worth.":** https://www.simonandschuster.com/books/Your-Network-Is-Your-Net-Worth/Porter-Gale/9781451688757
- **Ritesh Agarwal, Founder and CEO of OYO Rooms:** https://twitter.com/riteshagar/status/1676476120735293442
- https://www.forbes.com/profile/ritesh-agarwal/
- **Falguni Nayar, Founder of Nykaa:** https://www.forbes.com/profile/falguni-nayar/#:~:text=Veteran%20investment%20banker%2Dturned%2Dentrepreneur%20Falguni%20Nayar%2C%20who%20has,which%20she%20founded%20in%202012.

- https://yourstory.com/2023/10/the-mother-daughter-duo-building-a-lifestyle-empire#:~:text=Falguni%20Nayar's%20wisdom%20and%20experience,formidable%20cosmetics%20and%20fashion%20business&text=Nykaa%20founder%20Falguni%20Nayar's%20entrepreneurial,freedom%20to%20pursue%20her%20dreams.

- **The Importance of Online Presence for Personal Branding**: https://www.linkedin.com/advice/3/how-important-personal-brand-your-online-presence-jlfxc

- https://www.personalbrandingblog.com/

- **Mastering Personal Branding and Networking for Success**: https://remotereactor.com/blog/personal-branding-and-networking/

- **The Digital Presence Influence Model (DPIM)**: https://www.researchgate.net/publication/373452880_Enhancing_Digital_Presence_Local_Businesses_A_Social_Media_Marketing_and_Digital_Marketing_Internship_at_Pencil_Designers_Submitted_By_Under_the_guidance_of_Mr_Mahesh_Motwani_Pencil_Designers

- Online Learning and Professional Development:

- https://www.coursera.org/en-INrsera

- https://www.edx.org/

- https://www.udemy.com/

- https://www.linkedin.com/learning/

- https://www.khanacademy.org/

- https://skillshop.withgoogle.com/

- https://online.hbs.edu/courses/

- **Boost Your Career Resiliency with Your Personal Brand**: https://www.bcmanagement.com/post/boost-your-career-resiliency-with-your-personal-brand

- **Resilience and Personal Branding**: https://www.lettermanwhite.com/lwc-insights/resilience-and-your-personal-brand

- **Building Resilient Leadership**: https://www.thnk.org/blog/resilient-leadership/

- **Developing Emotional Resilience**: https://www.forbes.com/sites/jiawertz/2024/04/22/keys-to-building-resilience-for-personal-and-professional-growth/

- **Resilience in Professional Development**: https://hbr.org/2016/06/627-building-resilience-ic-5-ways-to-build-your-personal-resilience-at-work

- **Understanding the Importance of Personal Branding and Reinvention**: https://www.linkedin.com/pulse/reinventing-yourself-through-personal-branding-guide-vandana-nanda-#:~:text=Personal%20branding%20goes%20beyond%20logos,new%20identity%20with%20your%20goals.

- https://hbr.org/2011/03/reinventing-your-personal-brand

- **Role of Upskilling and Continuous Learning**: https://www.forbes.com/sites/karadennison/2023/04/13/the-importance-of-upskilling-and-continuous-learning-in-2023/

- https://hbr.org/2022/01/how-to-build-a-successful-upskilling-program

- **Case Studies of Successful Reinvention**: https://thecomebackcoach.wordpress.com/2024/06/11/need-branding-help/

- **The Role of Networking in Personal Branding**: https://thecomebackcoach.wordpress.com/2024/06/11/need-branding-help/

- **Building Trust and Credibility through Consistency**: https://fastercapital.com/topics/building-trust-and-credibility-through-consistency.html#:~:text=Consistency%20plays%20a%20crucial%20role,strengthens%20the%20brand%2Dcustomer%20relationship.

- **Projecting Authority and Expertise**: https://cubo.to/blog/the-importance-of-consistency-in-personal-branding/#:~:text=online%20and%20offline.-,Consistency%20is%20key%20when%20it%20comes%20to%20personal%20branding%2C%20as,to%20yourself%20and%20your%20values.

- **Creating a Cohesive Brand Identity**: https://brand.education/the-role-of-consistency-in-personal-branding-and-personal-success/

- **Engaging with Your Audience**: https://cubo.to/blog/the-importance-of-consistency-in-personal-branding/#:~:text=online%20and%20offline.-,Consistency%20is%20key%20when%20it%20comes%20to%20personal%20branding%2C%20as,to%20yourself%20and%20your%20values.

- https://www.personalbrandingblog.com/position-yourself-for-the-career-you-want-not-the-job-you-have/

- **Digital Transformation in Personal Branding**: https://digitaldefynd.com/IQ/ai-use-for-personal-branding/#:~:text=SEO%20Optimization,and%20other%20essential%20SEO%20factors.

* **Authenticity and Personalization**: https://www.forbes.com/sites/karadennison/2023/12/18/the-importance-of-curating-an-authentic-personal-brand-in-2024/

* https://bootcamp.uxdesign.cc/the-importance-of-authenticity-in-personal-branding-253fc871fc7b